First published in 1951, *The Catcher in the Rye* continues to be one of the most popular novels ever written as well as one of the most frequently banned books in the United States. In his introduction to this volume, Jack Salzman discusses the history of the novel's composition and publication, the mixed reception it has received from critics and scholars, the arguments surrounding the attempts at censorship, and its position in a postmodernist literary world. The essays that follow focus on various aspects of the novel: its ideology within the context of the cold war, its portrait of a particular subculture within American society, its account of patterns of adolescent crisis, and its rich and complex narrative structure.

NEW ESSAYS ON
THE CATCHER IN THE RYE

★ The American Novel ★

GENERAL EDITOR

Emory Elliott
University of California, Riverside

Other books in the series:
*New Essays on The Scarlet Letter*
*New Essays on The Great Gatsby*
*New Essays on Adventures of Huckleberry Finn*
*New Essays on Moby-Dick*
*New Essays on Uncle Tom's Cabin*
*New Essays on The Red Badge of Courage*
*New Essays on The Sun Also Rises*
*New Essays on The American*
*New Essays on Light in August*
*New Essays on Invisible Man*
*New Essays on The Awakening*
*New Essays on The Portrait of a Lady*
*New Essays on Native Son*
*New Essays on The Grapes of Wrath*
*New Essays on A Farewell to Arms*
*New Essays on Winesburg, Ohio*
*New Essays on Their Eyes Were Watching God*
*New Essays on The Rise of Silas Lapham*
*New Essays on Sister Carrie*
*New Essays on The Crying of Lot 49*
*New Essays on White Noise*

# *New Essays on*
# *The Catcher in the Rye*

*Edited by*

*Jack Salzman*

*The right of the University of Cambridge to print and sell all manner of books was granted by Henry VIII in 1534. The University has printed and published continuously since 1584.*

CAMBRIDGE UNIVERSITY PRESS

*Cambridge*

*New York Port Chester Melbourne Sydney*

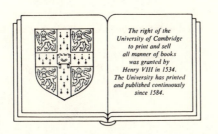

Published by the Press Syndicate of the University of Cambridge
The Pitt Building, Trumpington Street, Cambridge CB2 1RP
40 West 20th Street, New York, NY 10011, USA
10 Stamford Road, Oakleigh, Melbourne 3166, Australia



First published 1991

Printed in the United States of America

*Library of Congress Cataloging-in-Publication Data*

New essays on the Catcher in the Rye / edited by Jack Salzman.
p. cm. – (The American novel)
ISBN 0-521-37442-1. – ISBN 0-521-37798-6 (pbk.)
1. Salinger, J. D. (Jerome David), 1919– Catcher in the rye.
I. Salzman, Jack. II. Series.
PS3537.A426C357 1991
813'.54–dc20 91-29359

A catalogue record for this book is available from the British Library.

ISBN 0-521-37442-1 hardback
ISBN 0-521-37798-6 paperback

# Contents

# Series Editor's Preface

In literary criticism the last twenty-five years have been particularly fruitful. Since the rise of the New Criticism in the 1950s, which focused attention of critics and readers upon the text itself – apart from history, biography, and society – there has emerged a wide variety of critical methods which have brought to literary works a rich diversity of perspectives: social, historical, political, psychological, economic, ideological, and philosophical. While attention to the text itself, as taught by the New Critics, remains at the core of contemporary interpretation, the widely shared assumption that works of art generate many different kinds of interpretation has opened up possibilities for new readings and new meanings.

Before this critical revolution, many American novels had come to be taken for granted by earlier generations of readers as having an established set of recognized interpretations. There was a sense among many students that the canon was established and that the larger thematic and interpretative issues had been decided. The task of the new reader was to examine the ways in which elements such as structure, style, and imagery contributed to each novel's acknowledged purpose. But recent criticism has brought these old assumptions into question and has thereby generated a wide variety of original, and often quite surprising, interpretations of the classics, as well as of rediscovered novels such as Kate Chopin's *The Awakening,* which has only recently entered the canon of works that scholars and critics study and that teachers assign their students.

The aim of The American Novel Series is to provide students of

American literature and culture with introductory critical guides to American novels now widely read and studied. Each volume is devoted to a single novel and begins with an introduction by the volume editor, a distinguished authority on the text. The introduction presents details of the novel's composition, publication, history, and contemporary reception, as well as a survey of the major critical trends and readings from first publication to the present. This overview is followed by four or five original essays, specifically commissioned from senior scholars of established reputation and from outstanding younger critics. Each essay presents a distinct point of view, and together they constitute a forum of interpretative methods and of the best contemporary ideas on each text.

It is our hope that these volumes will convey the vitality of current critical work in American literature, generate new insights and excitement for students of the American novel, and inspire new respect for and new perspectives upon these major literary texts.

Emory Elliott
University of California, Riverside

# 1

# Introduction

JACK SALZMAN

## I

IN 1959, eight years after the publication of *The Catcher in the Rye*, Arthur Mizener began a *Harper's* magazine essay about J. D. Salinger by noting that he was "probably the most avidly read author of any serious pretensions of his generation." There were good reasons why this should be the case, Mizener commented. Whatever limitations the work might have had – either of technique or of subject matter – within these limitations it was "the most interesting fiction that has come along for some time."[1] Although, as we will see, there was little critical agreement about what the limitations of *The Catcher in the Rye* may have been, there was little disagreement with Mizener's contention that Salinger was the most avidly read "serious" writer of his generation. Soon after *Nine Stories* appeared in April 1953, it made the *New York Times* best-seller list. By 1961 sales of *Catcher* were reported to have reached one and a half million copies in the United States alone.[2]

But Salinger's popularity did not go unquestioned. Although numerous scholarly articles appeared during the 1950s, and continued into the early 1960s, by 1959 at least one eminent critic, George Steiner, had attacked what he referred to as "The Salinger Industry"; and two years later Alfred Kazin joined in criticizing the author he called "Everybody's Favorite."[3] At the same time, voices very different from those of Steiner and Kazin continued to denounce Salinger's work, especially *Catcher.* In one of the earliest reviews of *Catcher,* T. Morris Longstreth, writing in *The Christian Science Monitor* for July 19, 1951, offered a view that continues to haunt Salinger's novel. It is a story, Longstreth began, "that is not fit for children to read." For although Holden is alive and human, he is also "preposterous, profane, and pathetic beyond belief." It is a matter to be feared and not taken lightly: given wide circulation, a book like *Catcher* might multiply Holden's kind – "as too easily happens when immorality and perversion are recounted by writers of talent whose work is countenanced in the name of art or good intentions."[4] It was not long before *The Catcher in the Rye* began to be banned from high school reading lists. And more than thirty-five years later, an editorial in the *New York Times* would call attention to the force of Longstreth's warning: parents in Boron, California, had persuaded the school board to ban *Catcher,* a not unusual occurrence. "That sort of stuff is forever happening to 'Catcher'," the editorial noted; according to an officer of the American Library Association, it is "'a perennial No. 1 on the censorship hit list.'"[5] Yet, removed from reading lists, banned from libraries, and increasingly ignored by critics who seem uneasy with both its technique and its subject matter in a postmodern literary world – critics who at times seem more interested in Salinger's whereabouts than in his writings[6] – the novel remains one of the most popular, and more importantly one of the most read, of all works of modern fiction.

## II

For some, Salinger's popularity may have to do with his elusiveness and silence. He has, after all, published no fiction since 1966, and he has steadfastly refused to talk or write about his life (and, indeed, apparently has done all he can to keep others from invading his privacy). But the autobiographical enterprise, the need to find the writer in his or her work, to see fiction not as fact or history but as autobiography, is always of dubious value. There may well be, as one critic has written, "a public hungry to possess the famously elusive J. D. Salinger."[7] But surely the public that continues to read *The Catcher in the Rye,* even that part of the public which demands that the book not be read, is more concerned with the fiction written than with the man in New Hampshire who may or may not be writing more stories.

Just how much of Salinger one can find in his fiction – that is, how many scenes and characters have cognates in actual events and people in Salinger's own life – is at best unclear. (How much of Salinger is in Holden – or in Seymour or Buddy Glass?) What *is* clear is that well before the publication of *Catcher* on July 16, 1951, Salinger was thinking about the type of character who would become Holden. Just how far back the origins of Holden can be traced is hard to determine. Although Salinger did some writing at Valley Forge Military Academy and later at Ursinus College (where he enrolled in 1938 but stayed only nine weeks), there is nothing of any consequence in that work. Not long after he left Ursinus, however, Salinger enrolled in Whit Burnett's short-story writing class at Columbia University. There, as a class assignment, he wrote a short story called "The Young Folks." There is nothing in this work that anticipates Holden either (although at least one critic sees in one of the characters a "thinly penciled prototype of Sally Hayes in *The Catcher in the Rye*");[8] but Burnett, who also was the editor of the literary magazine *Story*, offered to publish it. Salinger was paid twenty-five dollars, and "The Young Folks" appeared in *Story* in the spring of 1940.

In November of the following year – after stories had appeared in the *University of Kansas City Review* ("Go See Eddie") and *Collier's* ("The Hang of It") – Salinger sold what seems to have been his first story about Holden Caulfield to *The New Yorker*. However, the entry of the United States into World War II delayed publication of the story until 1946, when it appeared as "Slight Rebellion off Madison" in the December 21 issue. In the meantime Salinger had been drafted into the army, where he was trained for counterintelligence, landed in Normandy on D-Day, took part in five campaigns in Europe, and was discharged in 1945.

Several stories were published during those years, but none is of much substance. Even "I'm Crazy," which appeared in the December 22, 1945, issue of *Collier's*, is really of consequence only because it is the first published story to contain material that is actually used in *Catcher*. Nor were the stories published immediately after Salinger's discharge from the army significantly more interesting. A ninety-page manuscript about Holden Caulfield was accepted for publication by *The New Yorker* in 1946, but for reasons that remain obscure it was subsequently withdrawn by Salinger.

One of the two stories published in 1947, "The Inverted Forest" – the other was "A Young Girl in 1941 with No Waist at All" – is of interest now mostly because the story's central figure, Ray Ford, seems to foreshadow Seymour Glass in "A Perfect Day for Bananafish."

But it was not until the publication of "Bananafish" itself, in *The New Yorker* on January 31, 1948, that Salinger's stories began to show the consummate artistry that would make his fiction among the most significant produced by a writer in the post–World War II generation. In 1948, "A Perfect Day for Bananafish" was quickly followed in the pages of *The New Yorker* by "Uncle Wiggily in Connecticut" (March 20) and "Just Before the War with the Eskimos" (June 5). The following year "The Laughing Man" appeared in *The New Yorker* (March 19) and "Down at the Dinghy" in the April issue of *Harper's*. In 1950, perhaps the best known if not the best story by Salinger was published, "For Esmé, With Love and Squalor" (*New Yorker*, April 8); and earlier in the year, on January 21, Samuel Goldwyn Studios released *My Foolish Heart*, its disastrous version of "Uncle Wiggily." A year and a half later, on July 14, 1951, the *New Yorker* published Salinger's intriguing story of infidelity and self-deception, "Pretty Mouth and Green My Eyes." Two days later, on July 16, Little, Brown brought out *The Catcher in the Rye*.

## III

The earliest critical responses to Salinger's first – and what increasingly seems likely to be his only – published novel were, as noted earlier, somewhat mixed. Some of the reviewers were clearly impressed. S. N. Behrman wrote a lengthy and very favorable review in *The New Yorker*, and Clifton Fadiman, on behalf of the Book-of-the-Month Club, which had selected *Catcher* as its main selection for July, wrote, "That rare miracle of fiction has again come to pass: a human being has been created out of ink, paper, and the imagination." In a review that appeared in the *New York Times* on the day of the novel's publication, Nash K. Burger called *The Catcher in the Rye* "an unusually brilliant first novel," and Paul Engle, in a review that appeared on the previous day in the *Chicago*

*Tribune,* found it "engaging and believable," a novel "full of right observation and sharp insight." Other critics were equally enthusiastic: Harvey Breit, in the August 1951 issue of the *Atlantic,* commented that Salinger's novel "has sufficient power and cleverness to make the reader chuckle and – rare indeed – even laugh aloud"; Harold L. Roth, writing in *Library Journal,* noted that Salinger's novel "may be a shock to many parents who wonder about a young man's thoughts and actions, but its effect can be a salutary one. An *adult* book (very frank) and highly recommended"; James Yaffe, in the autumn issue of *Yale Review,* commented that "Salinger has written a book, with life, feeling, and lightheartedness – very rare qualities nowadays"; the critic for *Time* praised Salinger for being able to "understand the adolescent mind without displaying one"; Harrison Smith, in the pages of *Saturday Review,* called the novel "remarkable and absorbing . . . a book to be read thoughtfully and more than once"; and Dan Wickenden, in a review titled "Clear-Sighted Boy" showed his own clear-sightedness by calling *Catcher* a modern picaresque novel similar to *Adventures of Huckleberry Finn* and suggesting that it too might become a classic.[9]

Other reviewers were less enthusiastic. In *The New Republic,* Anne L. Goodman called *Catcher* "a brilliant tour-de-force," but felt that in a writer of "Salinger's undeniable talent one expects something more." Similarly, Ernest Jones, writing in *The Nation,* found that although *Catcher* was always lively in its parts, the book as a whole was "predictable and boring." Virgilia Peterson, writing in the *New York Herald Tribune,* expressed misgivings about Salinger's language: the novel "repeats and repeats, like an incantation, the pseudo-natural cadences of a flat, colloquial prose which at best, banked down and understated, has a truly moving impact and at worst is casually obscene." In England, where *Catcher* was published in August by Hamish Hamilton, the critic for the *Times Literary Supplement* also had a mixed response: Holden is "very touching," but "the endless stream of blasphemy and obscenity in which he talks, credible as it is, palls after the first chapter."[10]

Even less enthusiastic were the notices that appeared in *Catholic World* and *Commentary.* Riley Hughes, in *Catholic World,* adopting a position not unlike that of T. Morris Longstreth in *The Christian*

*Science Monitor,* condemned the novel's "excessive use of amateur swearing and coarse language," which he argued made Holden's iconoclastic character "monotonous and phony." Even more critical was a review by William Poster that appeared in the January 1952 issue of *Commentary:* "The ennui, heartburn, and weary revulsions of *The Catcher in the Rye,*" Poster wrote, "are the inevitable actions, not of an adolescent, however disenchanted, but of a well-paid satirist with a highly developed technique, no point of view, and no target to aim at but himself."[11]

## IV

The initial critical response to *Catcher in the Rye,* then, certainly was not remarkable. The few critics who regarded the novel as "a brilliant performance and in its own way just about flawless"[12] were more than offset by reviewers who had serious reservations about the novel's worth. But the book sold well, if not remarkably so. Within two weeks of its publication, *The Catcher in the Rye* made its way on to the *New York Times* best-seller list, where it remained for almost thirty weeks. During this time, however, it never moved higher than fourth place, and failed to attain the success of Herman Wouk's *The Caine Mutiny,* James Jones's *From Here to Eternity,* James Michener's *Return to Paradise,* or Nicholas Monsarrat's *The Cruel Sea.* On March 2, 1952, *Catcher* made its last appearance on the list, in twelfth place.[13]

Even after *The Catcher in the Rye* lost its position on the best-seller list, Salinger was not long out of the public eye (though he would try to become so by moving from Westport, Connecticut, to the more private surroundings of Cornish, New Hampshire). On April 6, 1953, a little more than a year after *Catcher*'s disappearance from the best-seller list, Little, Brown brought out the first collection of Salinger's short fiction, *Nine Stories* (all previously published, and all but two – "Down at the Dinghy" and "De Daumier-Smith's Blue Period" – having originally appeared in *The New Yorker*).[14] Again, the critical response was somewhat uneven. A few critics complained that however great their insight, the stories were "little more than specialized reporting" or thought Salinger guilty of "a dodging of issues." But, in an important review in the *New York*

*Times,* Eudora Welty praised the collection, noting especially Salinger's ability to honor with a loving heart "what is unique and precious in each person on earth." Welty's endorsement was joined by such highly regarded literary critics as Gilbert Highet ("There is not a failure in the book; I would rather read a collection like this than many a novel which is issued with more fanfare.") and Arthur Mizener (unlike *Catcher, Nine Stories* has "a controlling intention which is at once complex enough for Mr. Salinger's awareness and firm enough to give it purpose"), as well as by critics for *Kirkus* and the *Chicago Sun Tribune.*[15] It was not long before *Nine Stories* was on the best-seller list, where it stayed among the top twenty books for three months.

At the same time, *The Catcher in the Rye* was attracting new audiences. By 1954 the novel was not only available in translation in Denmark, Germany, France, Israel, Italy, Japan, Sweden, Switzerland, and the Netherlands; even more significantly, it was made available in paperback by the New American Library, thereby beginning *Catcher*'s long involvement with high school and college students.[16] Yet despite his increasing popularity – or perhaps because of it – Salinger continued to shy away from any encounter with his widening audience. He not only insisted that his picture be removed from the jacket of the Little, Brown edition of *Catcher;* he also refused to comment on either his marriage to Claire Douglas on February 17, 1955, or on the birth of their daughter, Margaret Ann, in December of that year.

What Salinger did do was write more stories. "Franny" and "Raise High the Roof Beam, Carpenters" both appeared in *The New Yorker* in 1955 (on January 29 and November 19, respectively). "Zooey" was published two years later (*The New Yorker,* May 4, 1957) and "Seymour: An Introduction" two years after that (*The New Yorker,* June 6, 1959). In 1960, a son, Matthew, was born to the Salingers. The following year, on September 14, *Franny and Zooey* was published. Within two weeks, 125,000 copies had been sold, and for six months the thin volume remained on the *New York Times* best-seller list. Yet, despite his popularity, Salinger's world was becoming increasingly unsettled.

For some, Salinger's obsession with Eastern philosophy was a clear indication of his troubled state; for others, the end of his marriage in 1967 was a more obvious manifestation of his personal turmoil. But, above all, something was wrong with the writing: nothing of any consequence was being published. The publication of *Franny and Zooey* was followed in 1963 by the publication in one volume of two previously published stories, *Raise High the Roof Beam, Carpenters and Seymour: An Introduction.* Two years later *The New Yorker,* in its issue of June 19, 1965, did publish another Seymour Glass story, "Hapworth 16, 1924." But this long, rambling story found little critical favor when it appeared, and it has never been reissued. Whatever the cause of the artistic failure of "Hapworth 16, 1924," it is the last work we have by Salinger. The rest, as critic and scholar alike have noted for the past twenty-five years, has been silence.

The silence, of course, has been primarily Salinger's. Yet despite the continued popularity of *The Catcher in the Rye* with students, critics have become relatively silent about the novel; Salinger's fiction no longer attracts the critical attention it once did. Indeed, beginning in 1965, the year when Salinger published his last story in *The New Yorker,* there has been a steady decline in critical interest in Salinger's work.

Not that the initial critical and scholarly response to *Catcher* was particularly striking. The first substantial essays devoted to Salinger's novel appeared in 1956. In "J. D. Salinger: Some Crazy Cliff," Arthur Heiserman and James E. Miller, Jr. set the tone for much of the criticism of the next ten years by arguing that *The Catcher in the Rye* belongs to major traditions of Western literature in general and American literature in particular.[17] "It is clear," they began their essay, "that J. D. Salinger's *The Catcher in the Rye* belongs to an ancient and honorable tradition, perhaps the most profound in western fiction. . . . It is, of course, the tradition of the Quest." In addition, they noted, American literature "seems fascinated with the outcast, the person who defies tradition in order to arrive at some pristine knowledge, some personal integrity." Natty Bumppo, Huckleberry Finn, and Quentin Compson are such figures; so, too, is Holden, only unlike other American heroes Holden "needs to go home and he needs to leave it." He is, Heiserman and Miller somewhat grandly proclaim, "Stephen Dedalus and Leopold Bloom rolled into one crazy kid." Somewhat more moderately,

Charles Kaplan limits his comparison to *Adventures of Huckleberry Finn,* arguing that both novels are concerned with "the right of the nonconformist to assert his nonconformity," and that Holden, like Huck, has earned his "passport to literary immortality."[18]

The interest in Huck and Holden was given fuller consideration the following year when Edgar Branch's thoughtful "Mark Twain and J. D. Salinger: A Study in Literary Continuity" appeared in *American Quarterly.*[19] Branch was not interested in revealing any influences that Mark Twain's novel might have had on Salinger's work. Rather, by looking at the two novels, he hoped to "bare one nerve of cultural continuity in America." For Branch, Huck's flight down the Mississippi and Holden's through the streets of New York are not very different: "*The Catcher in the Rye,* in fact, is a kind of *Huckleberry Finn* in modern dress." Above all, Branch concludes, *Huckleberry Finn* and *Catcher* "are brothers under the skin because they reflect a slowly developing but always recognizable pattern of moral and social meaning that is part of the active experience of young Americans let loose in the world, in this century and the last."

Years later, Mary Suzanne Schriber would publish an interesting attack on the views of critics like Kaplan and Branch. Her concern, in "Holden Caulfield, C'est Moi," is not with the comparison of Huck and Holden, any more than her attack is on Salinger or *Catcher* (which, she acknowledges, "perhaps legitimately deserves its popularity and its designation as a 'classic' "). What concerns Schriber is most readily seen in the ease with which Branch can speak of *Huckleberry Finn* and *Catcher* as "brothers under the skin," the unquestioned assumption on Branch's part – as it is on the part of Kaplan and most male critics – that the two youths speak not only for all adolescence but for the nation as well. *Catcher* criticism, Schriber writes, is guilty of androcentricity; "an adolescent male WASP," she reminds us, "is not automatically nature's designated spokesperson for us all."[20]

Schriber, of course, has not been the only critic to question the universality of Salinger's novel; nor has the gender issue been the only reason for the rejection of Holden as our designated spokesperson. In 1956, John W. Aldridge, writing about Salinger in *In Search of Heresy: American Literature in an Age of Conformity* (the same year as the publication of Heiserman and Miller's laudatory essay) echoed some of *Catcher's* original reviewers in expressing his reservations about the novel. Along with Kaplan and Branch, among others, Aldridge notes that *Catcher,* like *Huckleberry Finn,* "is a study in the spiritual picaresque." But Holden is not Huck; Holden "remains at the end what he was at the beginning – cynical, defiant, and blind." As for ourselves, writes Aldridge without explaining who "ourselves" may be, "there is identification but no insight, a sense of pathos but not of tragedy." Salinger may have made the most of his subject, but if so, his subject was not adequate to his intention. Nor, Aldridge harshly concludes, is Holden's world adequate to his contempt, and "that is probably because it does not possess sufficient humanity to make the search for humanity dramatically feasible."[21]

The vagaries of literary criticism are such that the year after Aldridge published his deprecating view of *Catcher,* Ihab Hassan produced one of the most positive – and balanced – essays yet written about Salinger. In "Rare Quixotic Gesture: The Fiction of J. D. Salinger" Hassan argues that Salinger has written "some of the best fiction of our time." Salinger's voice is genuine and new, if startlingly uneven. Hassan takes exception to the criticism leveled against *Catcher* by Aldridge and others. To Hassan, Salinger's neo-picaresque novel is "concerned far less with the education or initiation of an adolescent than with a dramatic exposure of the manner in which ideals are denied access to our lives and of the modes which mendacity assumes in our urban culture." The book, finally, is both funny and terrifying: "a work full of pathos in the original sense of the word."[22]

Frederick L. Gwynn and Joseph L. Blotner, in the first published monograph devoted to Salinger, *The Fiction of J. D. Salinger,* continue along the lines of Hassan and of those critics who liken *Catcher* to *Adventures of Huckleberry Finn.* (The colloquial language, the picaresque structure have "exciting resemblances"; even the ending of *Catcher* is as artistically weak as that of *Huckleberry Finn,* and as "humanly satisfying.") But it is Jesus Christ, not Huckleberry Finn, to whom Gwynn and Blotner want to compare Holden. Holden, the reader must realize, is a saintly Christian person. And although the reader is then told that there is no need to call Holden a Christ figure, the reader is also told just a few lines later that "Jesus and Holden Caulfield truly love their neighbors, especially the poor in goods, appearance, and spirit."[23] The idea of Holden-as-saint was to prove appealing to many critics. But to others, like Maxwell Geismar, Holden is little more than a "sad little screwed-up hero," who if he really is meant to represent the nonconformist attitudes of the 1950s, "is a rebel without a past, apparently, and without a cause."[24]

Despite the misgivings of such critics as Geismar and Aldridge, not only did *The Catcher in the Rye* continue to attract critical attention, but as the 1950s drew to a close few would have argued with Granville Hicks's contention in the *Saturday Review* that there are "millions of young Americans who feel closer to Salinger than to any other writer."[25] Yet Salinger's very popularity continued to be a source of concern to some critics. The novelist and critic Harvey Swados, also writing in the *Saturday Review*, expressed dismay at the outpouring of articles, essays, and speculations about the writer he called the "Greta Garbo of American letters." Salinger unquestionably is a clever writer, with a first-rate ear for the mannerisms of speech peculiar to the young; but after that has been said, "we find ourselves shifting, so to speak, from one foot to the other."[26] So, too, George Steiner, writing in *The Nation* in 1959, who attacks what he feels has become "The Salinger Industry."[27] Salinger, Steiner writes, is a gifted writer with "one excellent short novel and a number of memorable stories to his credit," who has "a marvelous ear for the semiliterate meanderings of the adolescent mind." He is, however, neither Molière nor Chekhov nor Mark Twain. Why, then, the adulation and the proliferation of criticism? To Swados, it was largely due to the "cult of personality" from which American letters was suffering. To Steiner it was due both to the failure of the critic's sensibility and to the need young academics had to publish if they were not to perish. "American literary criticism has become a vast machine in constant need of raw material," Steiner wrote. It is not that Salinger was not worthy of discussion; it was the language of that discussion – the pomp and circumstance of final estimation – that troubled him. By all means, Steiner concluded his telling piece, "let us have Esme, Daumier-Smith, and all the Glasses. But let us not regard them as the house of Atreus reborn."

Needless to say, the denouncements by Swados and Steiner changed nothing. Nor did Alfred Kazin's consideration in the *Atlantic Monthly*, in which Salinger, "Everybody's Favorite" author, is described as "cute" (no other word, Kazin writes, "so accurately typifies the self-conscious charm and prankishness" of Salinger's fiction) and *The Catcher in the Rye* as a work "so full of Holden's cute speech and cute innocence and cute lovingness for his own family that one must be an absolute monster not to like it."[28] Despite all the caveats, *Catcher* continued to be read widely both in the United States and abroad, and Salinger criticism remained as active as ever. Donald Costello's 1959 essay on "The Language of 'The Catcher in the Rye' " was followed in the early sixties by interesting essays about Salinger by, among others, Jonathan Baumbach, Peter J. Seng, Carl F. Strauch, and Kermit Vanderbilt.[29] It was during this period that the first major study of Salinger was issued, Warren French's *J. D. Salinger*;[30] and shortly thereafter, in 1965, James E. Miller's insightful little volume on Salinger came out.[31] (Miller contends that "no serious history of post–World War II American Fiction can be written without awarding [Salinger] a place in the first rank, and even, perhaps the preeminent position.") It was also during this period – from 1962 to 1966 – that five collections of Salinger criticism appeared, as well as two special issues devoted exclusively to Salinger's fiction.[32] Yet by the mid-sixties there clearly was a slackening of critical interest in Salinger's work. The various anthologies of Salinger criticism were essentially reprinting the same material; the scholarly articles were decreasing in frequency; and above all, those articles that were being published had little to add to what had already been written.

This is not to say, of course, that since the mid-sixties Salinger criticism has either come to a halt or has been without value. Two new monographs have appeared – Kenneth Hamilton's *J. D. Salinger: A Critical Essay* (1967), and James Lundquist's *J. D. Salinger* (1979) – and Warren French has twice revised his early study of Salinger.[33] In addition, French has contributed a long, rather smug essay on "The Age of Salinger" to a volume on *The Fifties: Fiction, Poetry, Drama,* in which he not only contends that Salinger "imposed upon a tacky age the style that it lacked" but offers the rather remarkable observation that *Catcher's* popularity is due to the fact that "most people of the 50s resembled Holden Caulfield."[34]

Holden, of course, no more resembles "most people" of the 1950s than he does Jesus Christ. If comparisons must be made – even to point out, for example, how different *The Catcher in the Rye* is from, say William Golding's *Lord of the Flies*[35] – then there is a much truer ring to Helen Weinberg's contention that Holden's world is Kafkaesque, or to Lilian Furst's comparison of *Catcher* to Dostoyevsky's *Notes from the Underground.*[36] Similarly, if critics must offer a "full-fledged psychoanalytical" reading of Salinger's novel, then an argument is needed that is more convincing and pointed than James Bryan's contention that Holden has "designs" on Phoebe and that Holden's "association of sex with death surely points to some sexual guilt – possibly the fear that he or Phoebe or both may 'die' if repressed desires are acted out."[37]

So, too, with political readings of the novel. More provocative and stimulating than Bryan's Freudian reading of *Catcher* is the Marxist interpretation offered by Carol Ohmann and Richard Ohmann in 1976.[38] The authors argue that *Catcher* is, among other things, "a serious critical mimesis of bourgeois life in the Eastern United States, ca. 1950." But it fails to offer a viable alternative to that society; and, "informed by history and politics," it is here that the novel most invites criticism, and here too where critics have most failed to "identify the shortcomings of the novel's awareness and art." One of the critics most chastised in the essay is James E. Miller, Jr., who responded by saying that the Ohmanns were myopic and naive to believe that "the problems of a sensitive and perceptive adolescent moving painfully to maturity can [ever] be solved by restructuring society politically and economically."[39] In their rejoinder, the Ohmanns made clear how sharp the critical disagreement was and went on to say: "We are not arguing simply that Marxism leads to a better reading of *The Catcher in the Rye,* or any other text, than New Criticism does, or myth criticism or psychoanalytic, though we certainly believe that to be so. We believe that Marxist criticism has priority over, and in fact explains, these criticisms, because Marxism – not as dogma grounded in scripture, but as a dynamic and self-critical method – offers a better understanding of the world than any other body of thought and practice."[40] Perhaps, but for all their earnestness the Ohmanns fail to convince us that Marxism offers the best way of reading literature or that the strengths and weaknesses of a novel are to be gauged by its ideological stance.

## V

The exchange between the Ohmanns and James E. Miller, Jr. was a high point of Salinger criticism in the 1970s, and little that has come after has been as interesting. In the 1980s, to be sure, two important additions were made to Salinger scholarship: Jack R. Sublette's extremely useful *J. D. Salinger: An Annotated Bibliography, 1938–1981* and Ian Hamilton's often irritating and offensive but frequently valuable "biography," *In Search of J. D. Salinger.*[41] But as the last decade of the twentieth century opened, and as *Catcher* began to approach the fortieth anniversary of its publication, there was little to suggest a renaissance of Salinger criticism. At the same time, there was little indication that Salinger was losing his reading audience, and even less indication that the censors were losing their interest in *The Catcher in the Rye.*

Indeed, censorship and *The Catcher in the Rye* are almost synonymous. There is no record, as far as I know, that marks the formal beginning of the censors' attacks on *Catcher.*[42] But the early reviews of the novel that appeared in *Catholic World* and *Christian Science Monitor* – reviews that condemned Salinger for recounting "immorality and perversion" – certainly set the tone for the formal censorship that was not far off. In 1960, for example, *Catcher* was removed from the library and the recommended reading list at a high school in San Jose, California. In Louisville, Kentucky, a teacher who proposed using Salinger's novel in his tenth-grade class was told that he would not be rehired, and the book was dropped from the reading list. And in Tulsa, Oklahoma, a group of parents insisted on the immediate dismissal of a teacher who had assigned what *Time* magazine in its account of the incident called "the most avidly admired novel on modern American campuses." The novel, the parents complained to the school superintendent, had "filth on nearly every page" and was "not fit to read." (After much debate, the teacher was retained, but *Catcher* was removed from the reading list.)[43]

In the ensuing years, the attacks on *Catcher* continued unabated, albeit not always successfully. In 1965, the president of a school board in upstate New York declared that *Catcher* was "dirty" and should not be allowed in any secondary school in the country. (In response, the faculty and students put on sale at a student book fair both *Catcher* and John Steinbeck's *Grapes of Wrath,* which the board president also wanted banned.) In 1972, a Kansas school district's advisory board voted unanimously to recommend that *Catcher* be removed from the district's approved reading list; the school board, however, voted against barring the novel.

Not long after, some parents in Massachusetts asked that *Catcher* not be allowed to be taught at a local high school. "It is totally filthy, totally depraved and totally profane," one parent told the school board. "I don't believe a young mind can absorb this book without being scarred." This time, too, the school board refused to ban the novel. But more often the novel has been banned, often enough by 1973 to be mentioned in the *American School Board Journal* as "the most widely censored book in the U.S." Indeed, so often has it been attacked by censors that when Anna Quindlen wrote a column in the *New York Times* in 1990 to express her anger at the attempted censorship of Robert Mapplethorpe's photographs, she began by pointing out that *The Catcher in the Rye,* "a great book, and a true one," gets "yanked out of American schools more than almost any other title."[44]

## VI

What, finally, is left to be said about this novel that variously has been called "great" and "true" as well as "perverse" and "immoral"? In secondary schools, colleges, and universities, it may well be the most widely read post–World War II American novel – and the most banned. For a few years, critics and scholars seemed as interested in Salinger's fiction as did undergraduates. More recently,

Salinger's personal elusiveness has provoked more interest than has *The Catcher in the Rye* or his stories. Every now and then rumors begin that a new Salinger work is to appear, but those rumors remain unfounded: Salinger's literary silence now seems even more definitive than his personal reticence. Yet despite his dismissal by some critics, his failure to publish anything in the last twenty-five years, and the competing popularity of such writers as Toni Morrison, Thomas Pynchon, and Kurt Vonnegut, Jr., *The Catcher in the Rye* retains a remarkable hold on our cultural imagination. Most notoriously, of course, there is Mark Chapman's killing of John Lennon, which is said to have been influenced by *Catcher*;[45] but there also is P. J. Kinsella's novel *Shoeless Joe* and John Guare's play *Six Degrees of Separation*, with their homages to Salinger, to make clear how firmly and deeply *The Catcher in the Rye* has influenced many of its readers.[46]

So, too, the essays in this volume: they not only make clearer for us why *The Catcher in the Rye* has had the impact it has; they also reveal the diversity of critical approaches to the novel. In "Holden in the Museum," John Seelye offers a personal response to the novel, whose pretext, he argues, is to be found in some of the early Humphrey Bogart films. Seelye places the novel within the context of the cold war, contending that it is a novel without an ideology but one which could be adapted to ideological purposes. In his essay "Pencey Preppy: Cultural Codes in *The Catcher in the Rye*," British cultural historian Christopher Brookeman also considers Salinger's novel in a cultural context, and he too recognizes the importance of movies in the novel. Brookeman, however, gives particular attention to people like David Riesman, Erich Fromm, and F. Scott Fitzgerald as he explores Salinger's portrait of a particular subculture within American society.

Joyce Rowe and Michael Cowan both focus on narrative issues in the novel. In "Holden Caulfield and American Protest," Rowe concentrates on the way Holden's form of alienation gains in significance when viewed both laterally and historically. Like Rowe, Michael Cowan focuses on Holden's narrative voice and on the conscious and unconscious strategies he employs as both character *and* narrator. In "Holden's Museum Pieces: Narrator and Nominal Audience in *The Catcher in the Rye*," he is above all concerned with

Holden's struggle to control his narrative as well as his audience. Finally, in "Love and Death in *The Catcher in the Rye,*" Peter Shaw argues that Holden's social observations and his psychological state are clearly interrelated. Whether one is interested in assessing Holden's mental state or his status as a social critic, Shaw insists that the reader must take into account the patterns of adolescent crisis.

My own response to Salinger and *The Catcher in the Rye* is somewhat different from those of the contributors to this volume. Salinger's best work – *Catcher,* "The Laughing Man," "A Perfect Day for Bananafish," "For Esme – With Love and Squalor" – is most impressive, I think, because it is *about* the failure of resolution, self-deception, and the moral consequences of such failure and deception. In 1966 Salinger told C. David Heyman that his interest in Zen Buddhism denoted his conversion to that which was "experiental and wordless. Its appreciation of life's absurdities and ultimate paradox defies any attempt to put it into words."[47] But Salinger's strength as a writer is not his appreciation of life's absurdities and ultimate paradox; rather, it is his struggle against such appreciation – such maturity. Holden, like the early Seymour, like John Gedsudski, Eloise, and Sargent X, does indeed reject the "phoniness" of the world around him. At the same time, those characters struggle with their own complicity in that world; their rejection of the world's corruptibility is meaningful primarily because they recognize their own corruptibility. The serious writer, as Joyce Carol Oates has reminded us, bears witness to "the complexity of the world, its evils as well as its goods."[48] Salinger at his best brilliantly bears witness to that complexity. But bearing witness to a sullied world, and recognizing one's own involvement in that world, may not allow for any meaningful response. Holden's wish to be a catcher in the rye, like his need to smash a window when he learns of his brother's death, may be all there is. The Zen koan that serves as epigram for *Nine Stories* asks, "We know the sound of two hands clapping. But what is the sound of one hand clapping?" Whatever the answers may be, we know what the answer must be: silence. When Salinger began to look for other answers, when indeed he began to find those answers, he began to lose his voice as an important artist. But while he struggled with that silence, with the absurdity and paradox of both Holden and the world in which he lives, Salinger's voice was as striking as any writer's of our time.

## NOTES

1. Arthur Mizener, "The Love Song of J. D. Salinger," *Harper's Monthly* 218 (February 1959): 83.
2. See Robert Gutwill, "Everybody's Caught *The Catcher in the Rye,*" *New York Times Book Review,* January 14, 1961, p. 38. Of the 1.5 million copies sold, 1.25 million were in paperback.
3. George Steiner, "The Salinger Industry," *The Nation* 189 (November 14, 1959): 360–3; Alfred Kazin, "J. D. Salinger: 'Everybody's Favorite'," *Atlantic Monthly* 208 (August 1961): 27–31.
4. T. Morris Longstreth, "New Novels in the News," *Christian Science Monitor,* July 19, 1951, p. 11.
5. *New York Times,* September 6, 1989, p. A24.
6. See, for example Ian Hamilton's quasi-biography, *In Search of J. D. Salinger,* (New York: Random House, 1988; rpt. Vintage Books, 1989). All references hereinafter to Hamilton's book will be to the Vintage edition.
7. See Christopher Lehmann-Haupt's review of Ian Hamilton's *In Search of J. D. Salinger* in *The New York Times,* May 19, 1988, p. 29.
8. See Hamilton, *In Search,* p. 57.
9. S. N. Behrman, "The Vision of Innocence," *The New Yorker* 27 (August 11, 1951): 64–8; Clifton Fadiman, *Book-of-the-Month Club News,* July 1951, pp. 1–4; Nash K. Burger, "Books of the Times," *New York Times,* July 16, 1951, p. 19; Paul Engle, "Honest Tale of Distraught Adolescent," *Chicago Sunday Tribune Magazine of Books,* July 15, 1951, p. 3; Harvey Breit, "Reader's Choice," *Atlantic Monthly* 188 (August 1951): 82–5; Harold L. Roth, "Salinger, J. D. The Catcher in the Rye," *Library Journal* 86 (July 1951): 1125–6; James Yaffe, "Outstanding Novels," *Yale Review* 41 (Autumn 1951): viii; "With Love and 20-20 Vision," *Time* 57 (July 16, 1951): 96–7; Harrison Smith, "Manhattan Ulysses, Junior," *Saturday Review* 34 (July 14, 1951): 12–13; Dan Wickendan, "Clear-Sighted Boy," *The Freeman* (September 10, 1951): 798. In England, Elizabeth Bowen wrote in the London *Observer* for December 30, 1951, that *Catcher* is "the novel about adolescence to

end all: here the potential of tragedy is given an enchantingly comic sheath" (p. 71).

10. Anne L. Goodman, "Mad about Children," *New Republic* 125 (July 16, 1951): 20–1; Ernest Jones, "Case History of All of Us," *The Nation* 178 (September 1, 1951): 176; Virgilia Peterson, "Three Days in the Bewildering World of an Adolescent," *New York Herald Tribune Book Review*, July 15, 1951, p. 3; "Young Minds," London *Times Literary Supplement*, September 7, 1951, p. 561.
11. Riley Hughes, "New Novels: *The Catcher in the Rye*," *Catholic World* 174 (November 1951): 154; William Poster, "Tomorrow's Child," *Commentary* 13 (January 1952): 90–2.
12. Wickendan, "Clear-Sighted Boy," p. 798.
13. *Catcher* first appeared on the best-seller list on July 29, 1951, fourteenth on a list of sixteen. On August 19, it was listed fourth, a position it held through October 21.
14. "Down at the Dinghy" was originally published in *Harper's* 198 (April 1949): 87–91, and "De Daumier-Smith's Blue Period" in *World Review*, no. 39 (May 1952): 33–48.
15. Riley Hughes, *Catholic World* 178 (June 1953): 233; Seymour Krim, "Surface and Substance in a Major Talent," *Commonweal* 57 (April 24, 1953): 78; Eudora Welty, "Threads of Innocence," *New York Times Book Review*, April 5, 1953, p. 4.; Gilbert Highet, "New Books: Always Roaming with a Hungry Heart," *Harper's* 206 (June 1953): 100–9; Arthur Mizener, "In Genteel Traditions," *New Republic* 25 (May 1953): 19–20; *Kirkus*, February 1, 1953, p. 80; Franny Butcher, *Chicago Sun Tribune*, April 26, 1953, p. 2.
16. *The Catcher in the Rye* was first reissued by Grosset and Dunlap in 1952. In 1953, New American Library published the novel in its Signet Books paperback line. Five years later it came out in the Modern Library series. In 1964 Bantam Books published *Catcher* in paperback; by August 1989 it had gone through sixty-nine printings.
17. Arthur Heiserman and James E. Miller, Jr., "J. D. Salinger: Some Crazy Cliff," *Western Humanities Review* 10 (Spring 1956): 129–37.
18. Charles Kaplan, "Holden and Huck: The Odysseys of Youth," *College English* 18 (November 1956): 76–80.
19. Edgar Branch, "Mark Twain and J. D. Salinger: A Study in Literary Continuity," *American Quarterly* 9 (Summer 1957): 144–58.
20. Mary Suzanne Schriber, "Holden Caulfield, C'est Moi" in *Critical Essays on Salinger's "The Catcher in the Rye,"* ed. Joel Salzberg (Boston: G. K. Hall, 1990).

21. John W. Aldridge, *In Search of Heresy: American Literature in an Age of Conformity* (New York: McGraw-Hill, 1956).
22. Ihab Hassan, "Rare Quixotic Gesture: The Fiction of J. D. Salinger," *The Western Review* 21 (Summer 1957): 261–80. This article was incorporated in expanded form in 1961 into Hassan's study of the contemporary American novel, *Radical Innocence* (Princeton, N.J.: Princeton University Press, 1961).
23. Frederick L. Gwynn and Joseph L. Blotner, *The Fiction of J. D. Salinger* (Pittsburgh: University of Pittsburgh Press, 1958).
24. Maxwell Geismar, "J. D. Salinger: The Wise Child and the *New Yorker* School of Fiction" in *American Moderns: A Mid-Century View of Contemporary Fiction* (New York: Hill and Wang, 1958), pp. 195–209.
25. Granville Hicks, "J. D. Salinger: Search for Wisdom," *Saturday Review* 42 (July 25, 1959): 13, 30.
26. Harvey Swados, "Must Writers Be Characters?" *Saturday Review* 43 (October 1, 1960): 12–14, 58.
27. George Steiner, "The Salinger Industry," *The Nation* 189 (November 14, 1959): 360–3.
28. Alfred Kazin, "J. D. Salinger: 'Everybody's Favorite'," *Atlantic Monthly* 207 (August 1961): 27–31.
29. Donald P. Costello, "The Language of *The Catcher in the Rye*," *American Speech* 34 (October 1959): 172–81; Jonathan Baumbach, "The Saint as a Young Man: A Reappraisal of *The Catcher in the Rye*," *Modern Language Quarterly* 25 (December 1964): 461–72; Peter J. Seng, "The Fallen Idol: The Immature World of Holden Caulfield," *College English* 23 (December 1961): 203–9; Carl F. Strauch, "Kings in the Back Row: Meaning Through Structure – A Reading of Salinger's *The Catcher in the Rye*," *Wisconsin Studies in Contemporary Fiction* 2 (Winter 1961): 5–30; Kermit Vanderbilt, "Symbolic Resolution in *The Catcher in the Rye:* The Cap, the Carousel, and the American West," *Western Humanities Review* 17 (Summer 1963): 271–7.
30. Warren French, *J. D. Salinger* (New York: Twayne, 1963).
31. James E. Miller, Jr., *J. D. Salinger* (Minneapolis: University of Minnesota Press, 1965).
32. The collections of criticism are: William F. Belcher and James W. Lee, eds., *Salinger and the Critics* (Belmont, Calif.: Wadsworth, 1962); Henry Anatole Grunwald, ed., *Salinger: A Critical and Personal Portrait* (New York: Harper, 1962); Marvin Laser and Norman Fruman, eds., *Studies in J. D. Salinger: Reviews and Critiques of "The Catcher in the Rye" and Other Fiction* (New York: Odyssey Press, 1963); Malcolm M. Marsden, ed., *If You Really Want to Know: A "Catcher" Casebook*

(Chicago: Scott, Foresman, 1963); Harold P. Simonson and Philip E. Hager, eds., *Salinger's "Catcher in the Rye": Clamor vs. Criticism* (Boston, Heath, 1963). The special Salinger issues were brought out by *Wisconsin Studies in Contemporary Literature* 4 (Winter 1963) and *Modern Fiction Studies* 12 (Autumn 1966).

33. Kenneth Hamilton, *Jerome David Salinger: A Critical Essay* (Grand Rapids, Mich.: Erdmans, 1967) and James Lundquist, *J. D. Salinger* (New York: Ungar, 1979). In 1976, G. K. Hall published a revision of French's 1963 study, and in 1988 issued yet another revision, this one titled, *J. D. Salinger, Revisited.*
34. Warren French, "The Age of Salinger" in Warren French, ed., *The Fifties: Fiction, Poetry, Drama* (Deland, Florida: Everett/Edwards, 1970), pp. 1–39.
35. For a comparison of the two novels, see Francis E. Kearns, "Salinger and Golding: Conflict on Campus," *America* 108 (January 26, 1963): 136–9.
36. See Helen Weinberg, "J. D. Salinger's Holden and Seymour and the Spiritual Activist Hero" in *The New Novel in America* (Ithaca, N.Y.: Cornell University Press, 1970), pp. 141–64, and Lilian R. Furst, "Dostoyevsky's *Notes from the Underground* and Salinger's *The Catcher in the Rye,*" *Canadian Review of Comparative Literature* 5 (Winter 1978): 72–85.
37. James Bryan, "The Psychological Structure of *The Catcher in the Rye,*" *PMLA* 89, no. 5 (1974): 1065–74. See also Dennis Vail's response in *PMLA* 91, no. 1 (June 1976): 120–1, as well as James M. Mellard, "The Disappearing Subject: A Lacanian Reading of *The Catcher in the Rye*" in Joel Salzberg, ed., *Critical Essays,* pp. 197–214. For an Adlerian approach to *Catcher,* see R. J. Huber, "Adlerian Theory and Its Application to *The Catcher in the Rye* – Holden Caulfield" in *Psychological Perspectives on Literature: Freudian Dissidents and Neo-Freudians,* ed. Joseph Natoli (Hamden, Conn.: Shoe String Press, 1984), pp. 43–52.
38. Carol Ohmann and Richard Ohmann, "Reviewers, Critics, and *The Catcher in the Rye,*" *Critical Inquiry* 3 (Autumn 1976): 15–37.
39. James E. Miller, Jr., "*Catcher* In and Out of History," *Critical Inquiry* 3 (Spring 1977): 599–603.
40. Carol Ohmann and Richard Ohmann, "Universals and the Historically Particular," *Critical Inquiry* 3 (Summer 1977): 773–7.
41. Jack R. Sublette, *J. D. Salinger: An Annotated Bibliography, 1938–1981* (New York: Garland, 1984). For Hamilton, see note 6.
42. In "Raise High the Barriers, Censors," *America* 104 (January 7, 1961): 441–3, Edward P. J. Corbett suggests that the firing of a teacher from

a West Coast college in 1955 may be "the earliest instance of a teacher getting into serious trouble over J. D. Salinger's book."

43. For the San Jose incident, see "East Side School Superintendent May Organize Book 'Reviewers'," San Jose *News,* April 26, 1960, p. 13. The Kentucky episode is reported in the *New York Times,* March 20, 1960, p. 85, and by Donald M. Fiene, the teacher involved, in "From a Study of Salinger; Controversy in *The Catcher,*" *The Realist* 1 (December 1961): 23–5. The trouble in Tulsa is recorded in "Embattled City Teacher Assured She'll Keep Her Job," Tulsa *Daily World,* April 26, 1960, p. 5, and "Rye on the Rocks," *Time,* May 9, 1960, p. 67.
44. The controversy in upstate Vestal, New York, was reported in the *New York Times,* March 7, 1965, p. 75 and March 28, 1965, p. 75. For the Shawnee Mission, Kansas, story, see "'Catcher' Catches It . . . Again," *Newsletter on Intellectual Freedom* 21 (May 1972): 88. The *New York Times* carried an account of the Salem, Massachusetts, struggle on October 11, 1977, p. 67, and November 9, 1977, p. 25B. Anna Quindlen's editorial, "Dirty Pictures," appeared in the *New York Times* on April 22, 1990, p. 27.
45. For a consideration of the role of *The Catcher in the Rye* in Mark Chapman's murder of John Lennon, see Daniel M. Stashower, "On First Looking into Chapman's Holden," *American Scholar* 52 (1983): 373–7.
46. As recently as April 1991, the writer Harold Brodkey spoke of Salinger's fiction as "the most influential body of work in English prose by anyone since Hemingway." (See the *New York Times,* April 27, 1991, p. 26.)
47. C. David Heyman, "Salinger IS Alive," *The Village Voice,* June 23, 1975, pp. 35, 36, 38–40, 42.
48. Joyce Carol Oates, "Why Is Your Writing So Violent?", *New York Times Book Review,* March 29, 1981, pp. 15, 35.

# 2

# Holden in the Museum

JOHN SEELYE

> I was the only one left in the tomb then. I sort of liked it, in a way. It was so nice and peaceful. Then, all of a sudden, you'd never guess what I saw on the wall.

I DON'T think I was alone, as a college undergraduate in the early fifties, in regarding Holden Caulfield as a royal pain, an affront to my generation, which was prone to assume supine positions in the name of material well-being. Most of my classmates were conformists eager to become Organization Men inventing Hidden Persuaders, and the grey flannel suit (with that touch of conformist flair, the tattersall vest) was our uniform of choice. Ours was the cause that James Dean's *Rebel* was without, and James's shadow figure, John Dean, was one of us. Our greatest fear was not of losing our individuality to corporate America but of losing our lives in Korea. Like Dan Quayle, we did our patriotic best by joining reserve units, hoping that the winds of war would pass by, leaving our private lives unruffled. About the time that Jack Kerouac was making his westward journey that would become thinly fictionalized as *On the Road,* I spent two summers driving from Connecticut to California to take part in a naval reserve training program that would result in an ensign's commission just in time for the end of hostilities in Korea. It was not me that Salinger's *Catcher* caught.

And yet it was during this same period that Holden's world-wary voice began to speak to multitudes of kids, many of whom took the hint from Salinger's much-regretted line about the kind of author you wanted to call up on the phone, and did. This phenomenal surge was, however, inseparable from the accompanying wave of course adoptions, by means of which the orphan-like Holden became the favorite child of the academy. Appearing the year after David Riesman's *The Lonely Crowd,* Salinger's novel would be assigned to his Harvard undergraduates as a casebook in point. English teachers were quick to catch the numerous allusions to Twain's classic and stuck the novel into the classroom as a kind of "Huck Finn II: The Sequel," illustrating the relevance of the picaresque postures of the American classic to adolescent attitudes of today. On a more sophisticated level, Salinger's novel provided an American counterpart to European existential texts like Sartre's *Nausea* and Camus' *The Stranger.* Thus Salinger's nonconformist tractatus became quickly co-opted by the curriculum, but with results no one could have predicted. By 1965, the college English teacher, peering through the clouds of tear gas on his TV screen, might well have wondered what the American *Godot* had wrought, for the very obscenity that Holden sought to expunge from public walls had become the symbol of the nonconformist Free Speech Movement.

As the agitation for civil rights in the South and dirty words in Berkeley melded with the outrage over the Vietnam War, college book lists were quick to join the fray, and Holden was joined by Yossarian and Billy Pilgrim, whose angst had a decided point. It was definably the Boy in the Red Hunting (i.e., Liberty) Cap who led the rest of the literary pack in arousing a nation of kids to a higher consciousness of universal fraud, acting as a transcendental Special Prosecutor of Adult Values and making straight the way for the protest movements of the sixties. But it was the Vietnam War that gave final shape and purpose to Salinger's tour de force, much as it lent fierce motion to a teenage mode validated and valorized by Holden's passive avoidance of phoniness, a generational nihilism waiting for something that would give it specific motive. It was the Vietnam War that converted Salinger's novel into a catalyst for revolt, converting anomie into objectified anger. Along with *Lord of the Flies,* which enlisted Anthropology I to give pigs a bad name, *Catcher* was a threshold text to the decade of the sixties, ten years after it appeared at the start of the fifties, a minority text stating a minor view.

But if Salinger's novel provided a prolegomenon to an intertextual sequence that flourished during the Vietnam era, as a catch basin of generational attitudes and artifacts, it is chiefly a repository for an earlier era. For though the novel may be identified with the antiestablishmentarian attitude of fifties intellectuals, who contributed to its popularity, as a deposit of cultural stuff it is demonstrably a product of the forties, the period during which *Catcher* was conceived and written. Incubated during the last years of the Second World War, published in the middle of the Korean War, and having had a definable impact on the literary context of the Vietnam War, *The Catcher in the Rye* is itself a war novel once removed, a subliminal war novel in which not a shot is fired but the process of conscription is well under way. That is the point I wish to make here, but let me start by sifting through the forties stuff of which the novel is composed, which will prove to be a time capsule of contextuality whose contents are a book of revelations prefacing the apocalypse of the sixties.

In returning to Salinger's novel after a hiatus of about twenty years, I was struck by the kinds of things I had forgotten, including some rather remarkable facts, like Holden's height – six feet, two inches – and his patch of grey hair, a Hawthornean blazon on one side of his head. We all remember the red hat, but the grey hair had escaped my memory, and I was, frankly, surprised by Holden's size, having thought of him as, if anything, shorter than average. Except for Frankenstein's monster, most of our archetypal outsiders are not known for superior physical stature, save in moral matters. But the most significant lapse in my memory had to do with what was clearly meant by Salinger as a meaningful characteristic, namely Holden's heavy smoking habit. He smokes several packs a day, according to his own estimate, and the story is spelled out by a steady exhalation of those cigarette-fondling schticks that used to be the standby gesture of every short story, novel, and movie script written in the good old days when there was a ready market, not a protest line, for stuff with a lot of smoke in it.

Most important, although Holden frequently dismisses movies with the same snarl with which he defines all the phoniness in the world (both identified with his older brother, D. B.), he has plainly seen a great number of them, to which references abound, and in several scenes he play-acts the part of a dying gangster, crediting the inspiration to "the goddamn movies." Since Holden associates smoking a cigarette with watching "myself getting tough in the mirror," there is a covert, even subliminal suggestion here of Humphrey Bogart as a role model. Nor is it too difficult to conceive of Holden as a first-person narrator derived from those hard-boiled detectives made popular by Chandler and Hammett, who wrote the books that became the movies that made Bogart famous. And since *Breathless* was *the* existential film, Holden stole one on Jean Paul Belmondo also (who actually *does* die from a bullet in the gut), for if *Catcher* is art, then it is Bog-art, and like the characters who made Bogart a famous image, Holden is caught in postures frozen in the forties. Besides the cigarettes and the world-weary pose there is the underworld into which Holden descends after he leaves Pencey Prep, a frozen time frame of 1940s nightclubs, floozies, and pimps, a world as seen over the back of a cab driver, starkly.

As I have already suggested, Salinger's novel is full of hints that its pretext is *Huckleberry Finn*, but as the specimen example which follows suggests, Holden is Huck with a definable difference, reminding us that the hard-boiled detective as a vernacular voice was filtered through a Hemingwayish seive:

> The cab I had was a real old one that smelled like someone'd just tossed his cookies in it. I always get those vomity kind of cabs if I go anywhere late at night. What made it worse, *it was so quiet and lonesome* out, even though it was Saturday night. I didn't see hardly anybody on the street. Now and then you just saw a man and a girl crossing the street, with their arms around each other's waists and all, or a bunch of hoodlumy-looking guys and their dates, all of them laughing like hyenas at something you could bet wasn't funny. New York's terrible when somebody laughs on the street very late at night. *You can hear it for miles. It makes you feel so lonesome and depressed.* (81, italics added)

I have added italics to the intertextual signals in order to emphasize their unlikeliness. Huck's ruminations on distance and lonesomeness are associated with his passage down river, and foreground his separation from life on the shore, where violence and corruption are the rule. But Holden projects his isolation onto the scene, and where Huck has his raft, his sanctuary, all that Holden has is the taxicab, the smell of which is a specimen piece of the scene around him, intensifying the boy's psychic nausea in confronting the adult world. It is, moreover, an intensely urban moment with no possibility of that pastoral refuge essential to the idyllic, idealistic moments in *Huckleberry Finn*.

Holden dreams of a Huck Finn–like asylum, a cabin in the woods that he would build after he went "somewhere out West where it was very pretty and sunny and where nobody'd know me," a place where "I'd have this rule that nobody could do anything phony when they visited me," so that if D. B. came to visit "he couldn't write any movies in my cabin, only stories and books" (198, 204). But it is only a dream (the asylum he finally finds "out West" is for the insane), abstracted like so many of Holden's fantasies from the very movies he condemns. He can find in the real world no sanctuary, no place to call his own, a dilemma that is not only adjunct to his existential angst but one that is warranted by what it meant to be a kid in the forties, for whom a car of one's own was just another impossible dream. It was *On the Road* that made the automobile an equivalent to Huck's raft, but then Sal Paradise is hardly a teenage kid and, besides, the car (like the raft) is borrowed.

But at least Kerouac's antihero knows where he is heading and what he is hoping to find, a romantic, even a quixotic voyage and one completely different from Holden's aimless, roundabout wanderings. Whether you style it a "quest" or a "flight," Holden's trip has no final destination, being a passage without a rite. Notably, Holden's hegira takes place between the time he leaves Pencey and the official date the school will be let out, a time frame he invents for himself and, being disjoined from adult or social chronology, a period with no identifiable place in any conventional context. Even at Pencey Holden has no privacy, having an obnoxious, intrusive roommate and an even more obnoxious neighbor, who is separated from him only by a shower curtain. When he flees to the city it is to public places, whether nightclubs or Central Park or the Museum of Natural History, and even in his hotel room he is visited by a whore and beaten up by her ponce. Only in Phoebe's bedroom does he find a temporary haven, and there only until his parents return and he is forced to hide in a closet, that traditional but insecure refuge of small children, burglars, and detectives.

Once again, Holden's equivalent raft is a taxicab, not a refuge from society but a specimen piece, which conveys him from one bad place to another and provides a companion who cannot give him the answers he seeks. This is part and parcel of the existential dilemma as defined by much fiction of the forties and fifties, whose heroes, like Bellow's Tommy Wilhelm, have no proper space or purpose with which to give themselves definition or identity. Moreover, Holden's tacit associations with Bogart elicit a similar generational coupling, for the first revival of Bogart's films in the late fifties coincided with the academic interest in existentialism and the mounting surge of undergraduate allegiance to Salinger's hero. Bogart's characters likewise not only have no place to go but nowhere to hide. Perpetually on the lam, they live in crumby hotel rooms, always alert for the threatening knock on the door, or in dingy offices with frosted-glass windows on which threatening shadows fall – temporary roosts surrounded by menace, the most famous of which is Rick's bar in *Casablanca,* about to be swallowed up by a war. And Bogart's heroes are besieged also by phonies and faggots, threats to their self- and manhood, those last refuges available to the portable hero, against which he revenges himself with his ubiquitous gun. The pistol is the ultimate response to corruption about which Holden can only dream, plugging "old Maurice" the bellhop/pimp in his hairy stomach with a nonexistent weapon.

Again, the Bogart connection reinforces the extent to which Salinger's is a novel deeply imbedded with forties materials and attitudes. Like the Bogart hero, moreover, the forties was a decade without a distinctive milieu, with very little to call its own, except the Second World War and the Willis Jeep. Cars, costumes, dances, furniture, movies, all were aftereffects of the thirties, furnishing out a long wait for the second explosion of popular culture in the fifties. Salinger's book, I think, draws terrific power from the emptiness of the forties, and if as a decade it was an afterimage of the thirties, then *Catcher* can be read as the ultimate thirties after-story, bereft of the usual social consciousness that characterizes so much fiction of the previous period. Rather than being sustained by some

W. P. A.–nourished vision of noble but starving farmers or by the proletarian-novel skeleton that sustains the urban context of a James Farrell or Nelson Algren, Salinger's is a story sustained by the movies of the thirties and early forties, most especially the kind of movie that pitted a noble-hearted detective against the filth and corruption of modern city life or transformed a dying gangster into a religious icon of social inequity. Dropping out of prep school, Holden drops through a crack in time into the reality of the world he knows through movies, and what follows is at once a privileging and a painful critique of the movie myth.

For Holden, the urban world is full of signifiers of adulthood, and he is less eager to rub out the Maurices of that world than he is to stop kids before they enter it, to enlist them in the fate of his favorite brother, Allie, whose mystic catcher's mitt is a creative token opposed to the screenplays written by his other brother in Hollywood. A moviegoer who hates movies, Holden mostly hates adulthood, from which he seeks to rescue all children, much as he wants all the girls he knows to remain virgins. There is of course only one way to escape growing up and that is Allie's way, which is why the book can be read as a lengthy suicide note with a blank space at the end to sign your name. The forties finally was our last great age of innocence, and Holden stands at the exit point, trying to hold everybody back from the fifties. Indeed, it is very difficult to imagine any role for him in the world of television and rock 'n' roll. He is intensely a forties kid, a movie kid, a Bogart boy, and the wonder is the extent to which he could nourish the kinds of kids brought up on television and the Beatles.

The original Holden in one of the early Caulfield stories is reported missing in action in the Pacific during the Second World War, but the boy in the novel is much too young to have served in that war. Still, he is seventeen in 1949 (or 1950, depending on your calculations) just the right age to be drafted into the Korean War, which is the only sequel we can project for Salinger's kid, an obit in a movie-screen epilogue, as at the end of *American Grafitti:*

> Holden Caulfield was declared missing in action in Korea.

Which is precisely the fate that awaited a number of kids who identified with Holden in the late fifties and early sixties, only (as after *American Grafitti*) it was in Vietnam. "I swear that if there's ever another war," says Holden, "they'd better just take me out and stick me in front of a firing squad," not because he is a war hater, but because he detests regimentation: "It'd drive me crazy if I had to be in the Army and be with a bunch of guys like Ackley and Stradlater and old Maurice all the time, marching with them and all. . . . I'm sort of glad they've got the atomic bomb invented. If there's ever another war, I'm going to sit right the hell on top of it. I'll volunteer for it, I swear to God I will" (140–1). If *Catcher* as a narrative is an extended death wish, then underlying that fatalism is an apocalyptic fantasy of self- and universal destruction, illuminating Mr. Antolini's intuition that "I can very clearly see you dying nobly, one way or another, for some highly unworthy cause" (188). We tend to forget the extent to which *Catcher* was written in the shadow of the Second World War, if only because there is scant reference to it, limited to an allusion to D. B.'s noncombatant experience in Europe – "All he had to do was drive some cowboy general around all day" (140). Yet D. B., we are told, "hated the war" and gave Holden *A Farewell to Arms* to read, telling him "that if he'd had to shoot anybody he wouldn't've known which direction to shoot in. He said the Army was practically as full of bastards as the Nazis were," an ideological neutrality not much removed from Heller's in *Catch-22*.

Holden's account of this conversation ends with the declaration by the mystical Allie that Emily Dickinson was a better war poet than Rupert Brooke, which leaves Holden mystified, but should clarify matters for us. Like Salinger, Dickinson is a death-obsessed writer, whose poetry virtually ignores the Civil War while laying out a bone field that is equivalent to a battlefield after the battle is over. If in D. B.'s declaration concerning the lack of difference between the U.S. Army and the Nazis we have a prevision of *Catch-22*, then in the dialogue between Allie and Holden and in Holden's terror of the army as the ultimate conformist zone we have a subliminal flash of *M.A.S.H.* and *Hair* that explodes into an image of gravestones all in a row upon row. That is, *The Catcher in the Rye* is a text derived from the forties whose post-text was the Korean and hence the Vietnam War. For in Holden we have a boy terrified of regimentation but eager for self- and societal destruction, a true anarchist for whom death is not only preferable to social restraints but the ultimate letting go.

Bogart's films of the thirties were likewise a subliminal preparation for World War Two, right alongside the C.C.C. camps and other New Deal phenomena of idealistic regimentation, conveying a message concerning the way in which a messy world could be cleaned up, an iconographic cluster centered by the figure of a man holding either a shovel or a gun. It was an idea that gained increasing momentum in *Casablanca* and the movie version of *To Have and Have Not,* featuring cynical American males suddenly motivated to take up arms against a sea full of Nazis. One of Bogart's earliest and lesser-known contributions to the war effort was *Across the Pacific,* set mostly on an ocean liner, with Sidney Greenstreet playing his antagonist, an American university professor so sympathetic to the Japanese people that he is willing to betray his own country. Greenstreet had already figured more famously as the epicene Fat Man in *The Maltese Falcon* (a story virtually without ideology), ironically sharing the name of the bomb that later devastated Hiroshima. *Catcher,* whose pretext is the earlier Bogart films, like those movies lays down the baseline for subsequent conflicts. It provides the rationale not for an anticommunist crusade but for the explosion against the Vietnam War by teenagers unanxious to have their hair cut and their private parts shot off, Procrustean measures associated with the repressiveness of regimentation. At the same time, underlying this anarchistic message there is the essential image of Holden wishing himself on top of the atomic bomb, which evokes that memorable image from *Dr. Strangelove* when Slim Pickens rides down the first shot of World War Three to its Russian target.

This dual nihilistic image is warranted by the pervading gloom of *Catcher,* a Wertherean weltschmerz that provides a threshold for twenty years of death and destruction, much as Goethe's classic of suicide came at the start of the Napoleonic wars. The greatest novel about the Second World War, *The Naked and the Dead,* was built on the thirties-prepared framework of proletarian fiction but with considerable dependence also on a thirties reading of *Moby-Dick* as an antifascist tract. The two most popular antiwar novels that appeared just before or during the Vietnam War, *Catch-22* and

*Slaughterhouse-Five,* were set in the Second World War, absurdist fictions that abjured Mailer's doctrinaire third-front framework for surrealistic expeditions into a fatalistic zone. *Catcher* likewise supplied not only the rationale for the antiwar, anti-regimentation movements of the sixties and seventies but provided the anti-ideological basis for many of the actual novels about Vietnam which have been and are still appearing, the early *Catch-22*–inspired fantasies having given way to the dreary, soul-numbing reality of purposeless combat in an empty wasteland of staring eyes.

In short, *The Catcher in the Rye* is as much a war novel as is *Moby-Dick,* despite the absence (indeed because of the absence) of an obvious target of bomb-bursting hatred. Appearing in the centennial year of Melville's devastating anatomy of American militaristic/technological culture, which set the whale hunt against the author's personal search for and despair about the meaning and purpose of life, *Catcher* takes place during the same holiday season and provides such an unlikely backdrop to Ishmael's departure. The advent of Christmas is used for ironic effect by both writers, reminding us that the first shots of our entry into World War Two (Salinger's war) also signalled the opening of the Christmas season. *Catcher* is a 'tween-the-wars story without a mad captain or a whale, but American events soon caught up with the book and made good the deficiency, sucking Holden right out of his dark and drizzly December into the maelstrom direct, as the "goddam carrousel" turned into a war machine and Phoebe burst into flame. And now, without a war to give it focus, *Catcher* like *Werther* declines into a tractatus for suicide, which is, as *Moby-Dick* and *M.A.S.H.* both suggest, a reasonable alternative to war, as kids armed with the pistols Holden didn't have hold back saintly rock stars from the corrupting influences of the world by shooting them dead.

## NOTE

Donald Pease, in his *Visionary Compacts* (New York: Cambridge University Press, 1987), has brilliantly demonstrated the parallels between the 1850s in the United States and the cold war of a century later. My own essay is obviously indebted to his insights. But where Pease shows the extent to which *Moby-Dick* is an ideological battleground, hence a dress rehearsal for the Civil War, my stress by contrast is on a novel without an ideology, the postures of which could nonetheless be adapted to ideological purposes once the occasion permitted. Again, the parallel instance is the character we associate with Humphrey Bogart as a screen actor, which in a movie like *The Maltese Falcon* has no ideological focus but a year later, in *Casablanca,* could be converted to a weapon of war. Greenstreet, similarly, who stands for societal corruption in general in *Falcon,* was easily translated into a salivating proto-facist in subsequent films.

Let me state here also my gratitude to my colleague Andrew Gordon, for a helpful critique of this paper in an earlier form, and to Michael Crocker, whose dissertation-in-progress on Vietnam War novels undoubtedly contributed to my reading of *Catcher* and its contexts.

All quotations are from the Bantam edition of *The Catcher in the Rye.* (New York: Bantam, 1964). Page references are provided parenthetically in the text.

3

# Holden's Museum Pieces: Narrator and Nominal Audience in *The Catcher in the Rye*

MICHAEL COWAN

> I should not talk about myself if there were anybody else whom I knew as well. Unfortunately, I am confined to this theme by the narrowness of my experience.
>
> –H. D. Thoreau, *Walden*

> Who knows but on the lower frequencies I speak for you?
>
> –Ralph Ellison, *Invisible Man*

> And what are you, reader, but a Loose-Fish and a Fast-Fish too?
>
> –Herman Melville, *Moby-Dick*

REREAD over the years as I've grown older and had to confront my own and others' varying reactions to the text, *The Catcher in the Rye* seems an experience in both constancy and mutability. What Holden Caulfield says of the Eskimo exhibit at the Museum of Natural History is equally true of the unchanging printed exhibit of Salinger's text:

> Nobody'd be different. The only thing that would be different would be *you*. Not that you'd be so much older or anything. It wouldn't be that, exactly. You'd just be different that's all. . . . I mean you'd be *dif*ferent in some way – I can't explain what I mean. And even if I could, I'm not sure I'd feel like it.[1]

Certainly Salinger doesn't feel like explaining what he means. He simply – or, rather, complexly – presents an encased or, if you will, frozen narrative fragment that bears some sort of analogous relationship to the Eskimo: "He was sitting over a hole in this icy lake, and he was fishing through it. He had about two fish right next to the hole, that he'd already caught. Boy, that museum was full of glass cases" (157). Salinger offers us no origins of the narrative, no "David Copperfield kind of crap," no story about how the Eskimo came to be fishing "in the first place" (one of Holden's regularly used expressions), or how the birds who in another case are always "flying south for the winter" (157–8) had gotten to be in the "north" in the first place. Just as the Eskimo's "case" both represents and freezes motion, so Salinger's text as a whole lays out a series of cases that rhetorically attempt to frame and freeze realities that at the same time we are asked to experience as dynamic and uncontrollable. As numerous critics have argued, Holden, as a character, confronts change as an unavoidable part of life while (as his name suggests) trying to "hold on," if ambivalently, to experiences and values not subject to change.

But the exhibits in both of Holden's museums do more than wrestle with time and its onslaught. They are tightly bound up with the problem of who controls what and whom, and by what means. The Eskimo in the Museum of Natural History may control two of the fishes he is eternally trying to (in Holden's language) "catch," but he himself is caught by the exhibit's unmarked creator. Similarly, the birds in another case may be eternally flying south, but they too have been caught by some artist in midair and forced, we might say, to represent the never-fully-to-be-realized escape from winter. Holden persistently asks where the Central Park ducks go in winter when the pond freezes. Do they die? Fly away? Get taken "away to a zoo or something" (8)? One possible answer offered implicitly by the Museum of Natural History is that they – or their representation – can be (in a double sense) preserved only by being placed on permanent exhibit, achieving a kind of ongoing "life" and even identity only because seen by generation after generation of audiences. Similarly, preserving the faces of the Egyptian mummies at the Metropolitan Museum of Art also involves freezing their "expressions" – making them available to new audiences by controlling, if not their full identities, then at least their personae.

Such experiences and personae, in other words, are being represented by what we might call a museum discourse.[2] Holden seems at least unconsciously to approve of the strategies and results of such a discourse – so much so that he himself relates to us a narrative that functions as a series of museum pieces: as a "long,

long room" of exhibits by means of which he tries, if not fully successfully, to control both the past of his memories and the present of his narrating by gaining at least partial control over his past and present audiences. In this context we may find suggestive Holden's comment that "I knew that whole museum routine like a book" (155). I will be arguing here that key elements of this "museum routine" are the conscious and unconscious strategies that Holden employs in the dual persona of character and narrator: a speaker who tries to preserve himself in part by maintaining control over a narrative that resists control and over an audience that may have in mind its own alternative narratives.

Although *Catcher* is of course a written document, Holden's narrative is represented as a spoken narrative. In both its diction and syntax, as Donald Costello and numerous other critics have argued, it offers us the "sound" and flavor of Holden talking. Holden is nothing if not a talker, perhaps even a compulsive talker. Even Holden's seeming reluctance, on the novel's opening page, to talk too much about some things ("I'm not going to tell you my whole goddam autobiography or anything") doesn't prevent him from talking nonstop from start to finish, without even a request that the reader/listener give him a chance to catch his breath. Such a performance in the present is consistent with his past performance in the narrative: as an actor in his own story, Holden has rarely been at a loss for *some* words, however appropriate or inappropriate to the particular situation. Whether with roommates or old teachers or sometime girlfriends or sisters or strangers, he seems nearly always to have something to say. When at a momentary loss for his own words, he can always – as a mimic of considerable skill – repeat back, in tones ranging from respectful to sarcastic, the words of his conversational partner. Or he can simply repeat his own words, even though he says he hates to hear others, like Mr. Spencer, repeat themselves. He may imagine pretending "that I was one of those deaf-mutes. That way . . . I'd be through having conversations for the rest of my life" (257–8), but he clearly can't resist having a long conversation – albeit a one-way one (a point to which I'll return) – with the nominal audience of his narrative. As he says in another context: "All's I need's an audience. I'm an exhibitionist" (38) – and, one might add, an exhibitor.

One important form his talking takes, in addition to the often-aphoristic generalizations with which he is perpetually embellishing the narrative, is the telling of stories, or at least fragments of stories. The narrative of his three days of wandering the previous December is, of course, by far the most elaborate, but that narrative in turn contains parts of other stories. As a character in his own narrative, sitting on the train with Mrs. Morrow, Holden concocts the embryo of a fiction about her son's turning down a nomination for president of his Pencey class (73–4). Talking to Sally Hayes at the Rockefeller Center skating rink, he includes her in a fantasy plot involving their life in the New England woods (171). But he also, in his role as narrator of, as distinct from actor in, the three-day experience, tells us about Ossenburger's Pencey visit and Edgar Marsalla's "terrific fart," about Jimmy Castle's suicide, and so forth. As many critics have observed, the content of his narratives – and, I would stress, their incompleteness – may tell us more about Holden than he realizes he's telling. But the very fact that he has undertaken these narratives at all may be the most important clue to his character and concerns.

It is possible to argue that, especially at moments when he is not having to cope with specific situational hazards, Holden's talk goes beyond the simply communicative, tactical, or therapeutic. At various points in his narrative he seems to derive considerable pleasure and energy – and a feeling of being truly "alive" – simply from the act of speaking. In fact, his talking seems at times to reflect less an interest in the *meaning* than in the *experience* of what he is saying. Holden seems to love the rhythms and cadences of his own voice, even self-indulgently so. His own creator, of course, is also enjoying the discourse of his creation (and enjoying himself creating the discourse), as do many readers. But I also believe it useful to locate such enjoyment in Holden himself, in both his acting and his narrating modes. Like another son of the Manhattoes, Walt Whitman, Holden seems at moments to find an almost unreflective pleasure in his own barbaric yawp, and uses virtually every occasion that confronts him – including the occasion of narrating his three-day tale – as an opportunity for exercising that yawp. (He's regularly being told that he talks too loudly.) If such exercise is in part his instinctive way of coping with the "lousy hormones" that the periodical he finds in Grand Central Station tells him are raging inside him (254), a sublimation, as the clinicians might say, of his pent-up sexual and aggressive urges, there is also a subtler aesthetic side to it, a side that causes Holden to respond to the little boy who has just come out of church with his family:

> The kid was swell. He was walking in the street, instead of on the sidewalk, but right next to the curb. He was making out like he was walking a very straight line, the way kids do, and the whole time he kept singing and humming. I got up closer so I could hear what he was singing. He was singing that song, "If a body catch a body coming through the rye," He had a pretty little voice, too. He was just singing for the hell of it, you could tell. The cars zoomed by, brakes screeched all over the place, his parents paid no attention to him, and he kept on walking next to the curb and singing "If a body catch a body coming through the rye." It made me feel better. It made me feel not so depressed anymore. (150)

Although the singing child becomes the inspiration for Holden's later fantasy of himself as a "catcher in the rye," the child himself seems to need no catching. Perhaps he is somehow protected from danger by the straight line in which he is walking, whereas Holden's love of digressions seems often to get him into trouble – make *him* the one who needs to be caught. The child's voice does just that – both catch Holden's attention and lift his spirits. Holden admits that "I don't read much poetry" (182), but he clearly responds to the sound of a poetic voice, and his own voice seems impelled at times by a poetic impulse. Maybe this impulse helps explain his relationship to the poems inscribed on Allie's outfielder's mitt. Holding the mitt brings him not only closer to Allie but to "catching" Allie's sensibility, including a poet's sensitivity to language.

Whatever its aesthetic or autoerotic pleasures for him (and for us), however, Holden's speaking must also serve him as a tool, if imperfect and often vulnerable, for surviving in a confusing, irritating, and even sharply painful world where poets get wounded and killed and things of value get lost. Although, during the three December days he describes, he seems to have had a lot of time on his hands – time potentially for walking along the curb singing to himself – his speaking voice is for the most part under the strain of ready alert, often evasive and forever preparing for combat. Sometimes his chatter is an index of his discomfort or nervousness in a particular situation, as in his encounter with the prostitute Sunny (123–5). Sometimes it seems an instinctive if often self-defeating tactic to help him gain some leverage over a situation about to veer out of control, as when he argues with Stradlater about Jane Gallagher (54–8) or tries to hold his own against the bellhop Maurice (133–5). Sometimes it seems a compulsive gesture to fill a fearful silence, an isolation that leaves him prey to his own lacerating thoughts – think, for example, of his talking out loud to Allie in his hotel room (129).

As these episodes suggest, Holden has often sought, if only instinctively, to derive at least some catharsis or control from the simple fact of having a listener, no matter what is said or how poor the listener, or how finally unsuccessful his attempt to communicate. Whether his talking to others has been sincere or "phony," whether it strikes us as comic or pathetic, whether it has momentarily soothed or simply further exposed his raw nerves, its partly conscious, partly unconscious tactical dimensions cannot be overlooked without our missing important clues to Holden and the novel. These tactical elements become further complicated when we consider Holden's implicit relationship to his nominal audience – an "interested" first-person narrator/character, both interested in the pleasures of telling his story and having a vested interest in the consequences of that story telling.[3]

By "nominal audience," I do not mean those of us who actually read *Catcher.* I mean the "you" inscribed by Holden himself – "If you really want to hear about it" (3) – as the listener(s) to his narrative. Surprisingly, relatively few critics have seemed particularly curious about this nominal audience, perhaps because there are things about it that neither Holden (nor we nor even his creator, for that matter) can know for certain. And yet the clues Holden offers about the nature of that audience may give us some clues to his own character, not only as a represented actor in the narrative but also in his persona as present narrator.

For example, Holden makes certain assumptions about what his listeners need to know about his world in order to understand it – "in case you don't live in New York," as he says at one point (184). At the same time, he seems to assume that his auditors know quite a bit about the place from which he is doing his narrating. In the opening and closing chapters he simply calls it "here" and "this crumby place" (3, 276). As to its institutional nature, he refers so casually to the fact that "I got pretty run-down and had to come out here and take it easy" (3), to the fact that "I practically got t.b. and came out here for all these goddam checkups and stuff" (8), and to "this one psychoanalyst guy they have here" (276) that it is not implausible for us to think of him as describing things his listeners already know something about. It is not implausible, in other words, to think of Holden as speaking face-to-face with someone seated in the same room with him – perhaps a visitor, perhaps even another patient. Furthermore, Holden seems to be talking directly to relatively few people – almost certainly to no more than two or three, and quite possibly to no more than one. We might remember that, as a character in the events he narrates, Holden is never seen talking to more than three people at once (for example, the three women in the Lavender Room), rarely to more than two (Maurice and Sunny, the two nuns, the two brothers at the Metropolitan Museum of Art), and usually to only one person at a time – the occasions, in fact, for his longest conversations (with Stradlater, Sally Hayes, Mr. Antolini, Phoebe). He seems most comfortable, and most verbally expansive, talking to a single listener, and he is clearly at his most expansive in his narrative from California.

It is also possible to infer some of the attributes Holden takes for granted in – we might even say demands of – his audience. His relatively unselfconscious resort as narrator to heavy doses of adolescent vernacular and his relative lack of straining toward a formal "adult" diction – the sort he uses self-consciously, for example, with Mr. Spencer or Mrs. Morrow – suggest a listener relatively close to his own age, one with whom he can feel both comfortable and not particularly deferential. He implies that he has already told one such listener, his brother D. B., "about all this stuff" (276) – or, at least, about much of it. Moreover, his putative audience seems almost certainly to be male. As a character in his own narrative, he has almost entirely avoided talking directly about sexual matters with women, whether older, younger, or his own age. Even with Sunny he is noticeably tongue-tied on the subject. At the same time, he can tell his present audience that Lillian Simmons "has very big knockers" (112) and describe his Lavender Room dance partner as having a "pretty little butt" (95). His preoccupation with sexual matters weaves in and out of his entire narrative, but his "male" talk stays away for the most part from macho posturings. Holden is able to admit to his listeners that he is still "a virgin" and to talk about his awkwardness and confusion in approaching women sexually (120–1). He would not have made such admissions to Ackley, Stradlater, or Carl Luce. Such reticence suggests another attribute of his nominal audience, namely its sensitivity.

In fact, Holden implicitly attributes several important virtues to his listeners. He clearly counts on "you" to listen respectfully and carefully to his narrative from the moment he starts talking until the moment he stops. The actual readers of the novel can, of course, put down the book whenever they wish. But Holden's nominal auditors, by the defining conventions of the text, are willingly caught in the continuous time required by his meandering storytelling. He can count on their never dreaming of "yelling 'Digression!' " at him, as his Pencey classmates did to Richard Kinsella (238–9). Equally important, he can rely on his listeners' intelligence. Most people may "never notice anything" (18) and "always clap for the wrong things" (110), but he assumes that the "you" will be like his sister: "If you tell old Phoebe something, she knows exactly what you're talking about" (88). Put another way, Holden clearly does not believe he is talking to a "slob" or even a "secret slob," or to a "phony." He trusts "you" to listen not merely perceptively but sympathetically to his admissions of past embarrassments, mistakes, lies, confusions, loneliness, and hurts, as well as to his present opinions and confusions.

In short, Holden seems to be telling his tale to listeners who in many respects resemble the kind of ideal audience that the narrator of Hawthorne's "Custom-House" essay imagines:

> As thoughts are frozen and utterance benumbed, unless the speaker stand in some true relation with his audience[,] it may be pardonable to imagine that a friend, a kind and apprehensive, though not the closest friend, is listening to our talk; and then, a native reserve being thawed by this genial consciousness, we may prate of the circumstances that lie around us, and even of ourself, but still keep the inmost Me behind its veil.[4]

Putting aside for the moment the question of whether Holden's talk reveals or veils an "inmost Me," we need not assume that, as a confused adolescent, he has the intelligence, insight, or wisdom to tell his ideal audience everything it (or the reader) might want to know about him and his experiences. There has been no dearth of critics to point to his mutually inconsistent opinions, the gaps between his professed values and his behavior, and his uneven insight into his own motives. But I believe it can be argued that Holden's verbal performance shows him eager, at least on the conscious level, to "stand in some true relation" with "you." Although he asserts that "I'm the most terrific liar you ever saw in your life" (22), that lying seems to have taken place mainly in the narrative past. Speaking in the present, he readily acknowledges those lies or makes them appear transparent. He seems trusting enough of his present "you," at least, to reveal many of his real confusions, fears, and hurts, as well as many – if not all – of those things he values most.

I stress the "presentness" of Holden's putatively ideal audience because of my belief that his representation of time is not only critical to his identity as narrator but integral to many of the novel's major concerns. Two of the most neglected complexities of Holden's performance as narrator are his relationship to his memories and, by extension, his audience's simultaneous relationship to his "pastness" and presentness. There are in *The Catcher in the Rye,* as in most first-person narratives, at least three "times" represented: the present of the narrating itself, the past that is being "remembered" and recreated or represented by the present narrator, and the even "earlier" past that is remembered by the characters (including by the narrator as a character) in the primary past being narrated. Thus, Holden is speaking to "you" from his own location in the present, in "this crumby place" near Hollywood. From that present location, he tells the story "about this madman stuff that happened to me around last Christmas" (3). Part of that story involves his recounting of the memories that he had *during* those days just before Christmas – memories of his brother Allie, Jane Gallagher, former prep schools he had attended, the Central Park lagoon and carousel, the Museum of Natural History and the Metropolitan Museum of Art, and so forth. At the same time, some of the objects of these earlier memories become the sources of new memories he has during the present of the narrating. From his present Los Angeles location, for example, remembering his clandestine December visit with Phoebe at the family apartment, Holden suddenly switches from past to present tense: "Finally, after about an hour, I got to old Phoebe's room. She wasn't there, though. I forgot about that. I forgot she always sleeps in D. B.'s room when he's away in Hollywood or some place" (206).

Keeping track of tenses and their temporal point of generation will help us deal with some of the major questions about which Salinger's critics have argued. For example, how much does Holden change in the course of the narrative? To the extent that changes occur, when do they take place – during the course of the three days at Christmas (and, if so, precisely when), at some time between that "madman" time and the time of the narrating, or during the course of the narrating itself? Such influential interpreters as Carl Strauch and James E. Miller, Jr., have argued that Holden undergoes some sort of transformative experience during the course of those three days, most of them placing it after Holden's traumatic experience at Antolini's apartment, and typically locating its key moments in his acknowledgment at Phoebe's school and in the Metropolitan Museum of Art that he can neither wipe out or avoid all the "Fuck you" signs in the world (262, 264) and in his rush of happiness while watching Phoebe ride the carousel in Central Park (273–5). Other critics, to the extent that they find any significant "recovery" at all in Holden, locate it in the period of his institutionalization, between Christmas and the narrating present. And a handful of critics suggest that it is Holden's present process of narrating that is itself the major transformative agent, serving him as therapy and catharsis.

I believe that close attention to Holden's tenses tends to support the views of those minority of critics who see relatively little permanent change in his character or insights in the actual course of his pre-Christmas wanderings in New York. Further, it is not at all clear that his several months in whatever sort of southern California facility he inhabits have altered his beliefs and feelings significantly. His stay there may well have given him a chance at physical recuperation and perhaps given his emotions the benefit of some temporary distance from that stressful holiday experience.[5] But, at least at the outset of his narrative, the opinions that Holden shares with "you" don't seem much different from the opinions he held, or reports himself as having held, during his December wanderings. In fact, Holden's present-tense opinions not only at the start but well toward the conclusion of his narrative seem about as stark as anything he represents himself as having believed during the New York experience. Certainly his irritation at others' phoniness and abuse of power is as strong when he looks back at Pencey and New York as it was when he first encountered such abuses. For example, he interrupts his past-tense recounting of Mr. Spencer's insistence on reading out loud Holden's paltry start at a paper on the Egyptians with a present-tense remark: "You can't stop a teacher when they want to do something. They just *do* it" (16). That Holden does not feel enough temporal and emotional distance from the incident to be mildly amused, or at least more charitably disposed, is reflected in his next present-tense comment: "I don't think I'll ever forgive him for reading me that crap out loud" (17).

Similarly, it is clear from Holden's explicit present-tense remarks not only that he has not gotten over many aspects of his Christmastime depression but that his mere remembering and recounting of things that exacerbated that depression reopen the emotional wounds. Of the remembered snobbery at Elkton Hills, he asserts: "It makes me so depressed I go crazy" (19). Remembering girls who come "all the way" to New York "to see the goddam first show at Radio City Music Hall," he states that "it makes me so depressed I can't stand it" (98). Of memories of somebody laughing on a New York street late at night, he remarks: "It makes you feel so lonesome and depressed" (106). Later in his narrative, still speaking from a California-based present, he comments: "When somebody really *wants* to go [to the movies] then it depresses the hell out of me" (151). If narrating his past experiences is supposed to be therapeutic for Holden, as some critics argue, there are relatively few signs of it in his present-tense remarks. Certainly such admissions do not seem those of an adolescent who has had a lasting cathartic experience at a Central Park carousel the winter before. Perhaps some of his views were modified or even reversed during the course of those three days – for example, the apparent replacement of his fantasy about being a "catcher in the rye" with a willingness to let kids fall off the carousel while grabbing for the gold ring – but, if so, some of those modifications have not survived the trip to California.

It is not that Holden's feelings don't undergo various changes in the course of narrating his experiences, but rather that those changes do not seem to move consistently in any particular direction. Indeed, it might be argued that, as Holden recounts specific remembered experiences, his original feelings and views about them are restimulated. Thus those experiences that angered or confused him at Christmas still anger or confuse him as he remembers them. Similarly, those experiences that amused him or made him happy at Christmas regenerate such amusement and happiness as he recounts them. In remembering his "epiphany" at the carousel, he has an epiphany again and can once again, in present tense, assert: "The thing with kids is, if they want to grab for the gold ring, you have to let them do it, and not say anything" (273–4). If so, it's not at all clear that the mood of that remembered epiphany lasts any longer than the instant during which he narrates it – lasts, in other words, long enough to significantly inform the tone of Holden's remarks to his present listeners in the final chapter. Although some critics have posited his achieving some sort of ineffable Zen-like or religious wisdom, he himself admits to ending his narrative with possibly as many confusions as he began with. He tells "you" what he has recently told D. B., when his brother "asked me what I thought about all this stuff I just finished telling you about": "If you want to know the truth, I don't *know* what I think about it" (276–7).

If it is not at all clear that Holden's remembering and narrating have brought him to an enhanced conscious understanding of himself and his past, what *has* his narrating achieved? Without trying to exhaust the possible terrain, let me venture two possibilities, one having to do with the "museum" function of his narrative and the other with the narrative's impact on his implicit relation to his nominal audience.

Let us first speculate that, in undertaking a narrative in the presence of an attentive, intelligent, and trustworthy audience, Holden is less engaged in exploring his past and learning from it than in storing it for possible future use. Holden clearly has a hard time holding on to and keeping safe the various things in his life, whether fencing foils, the record he buys Phoebe, or his brother Allie. His response to such losses – "One of my troubles is, I never care too much when I lose something" (117) – seems at least partly a rationalization. But the one thing that he is immensely concerned to preserve is his own experience. His memory functions as the cloth, with its "secret chemical," that he wraps around his mummies – people and moments he has loved and even those that have confused or hurt him. At the same time, his narration of those remembered experiences is a kind of attempt to place them on exhibit in a safe glass case. Thinking about the Museum of Natural History exhibits, he asserts: "Certain things . . . should stay the way they are. You ought to be able to stick them in one of those big glass cases and just leave them alone. I know that's impossible, but it's too bad anyway" (158). His refusal and/or inability to draw immediate lessons from those exhibits is equivalent to displaying them without affixing labels to them. In fact, one side of Holden actively resists such labeling efforts, or at least such premature labeling efforts. He complains that his Pencey Oral Expression teacher Mr. Vinson "could drive you crazy sometimes" by "telling you to *un*ify and *simp*lify all the time. Some things you just can't *do* that to" (240). In his oral performance for his present audience, Holden likewise resists the creation of such speciously simple and unified exhibits. On the other hand, he may unconsciously be following Antolini's advice to learn from previous morally and spiritually troubled men who "kept records of their troubles" and to keep his own record from which future audiences might learn (246) – perhaps including even Holden himself, as he grows older. His narrating may thus represent some nascent, fragile faith that he and future audiences will be able to return to those exhibits and find them illuminating, just as Holden keeps "thinking about old Phoebe going to that museum on Saturdays the way I used to" and how "she'd see the same stuff I used to see, and how *she'd* be different every time she saw it" (158).

The death of his brother Allie occupies one such case. As many critics have argued, that death may have been the single most traumatic event in Holden's life prior to his New York night of the soul after leaving Pencey. Its colors have in fact bled into so many other events – the deaths of Mercutio and James Castle, the Central Park lagoon in winter, the mummies in the Metropolitan Museum of Art, the "Fuck you" inscriptions on the school and museum walls – that they tend to blend in Holden's imagination into a master exhibit of the unjust cruelties of his society and the inescapable harshness of nature. More than one critic has suggested that his concern for the Central Park ducks reflects not merely his wrestling with the mystery and even seeming meaninglessness of death in general but with that of Allie's death in particular.

But Holden implicitly places at least one other set of materials in that case: his intricately mixed feelings about that death. If his grief over Allie's loss is genuinely deep and lasting, that grief also contains beneath its frozen surface some "secret goldfish" that Holden may unconsciously wish to protect. At one point Holden recounts to his listeners Phoebe's description, from a movie she has just seen, of a "mercy killer" (211). As with the doctor in the film, who tries to kill a crippled child to put her out of her misery and who "knows he deserves to go to jail because a doctor isn't suppose to take things away from God," Holden on some symbolic level seems to feel guilty about Allie's death. That guilt does not seem to spring from anything as obvious as repressed sibling rivalry: the jealousy "the dumb one" in the family feels toward a brilliant, saintly brother. Surely some of it stems from the fact that it was Holden who was spared while his more deserving brother was lost. But there may be another element in those guilty feelings – feelings that a twelve-year-old Holden is unlikely to have had at the time of his brother's death but that may well have surfaced more recently, as Holden has watched D. B., himself, and others "fall" out of childhood and become "phony." By dying when he did, Allie never suffered that fall. Retrospectively, then, Holden has acquired an ambivalent sort of vested interest in Allie's death. In order to preserve his image of Allie against the onslaughts of change, he has lovingly enshrined or "mummified" Allie in his narrative and thus, strangely enough, become symbolically complicit in his death. Thus, in recounting his self-punishing behavior at various points in his Pencey and New York adventures, Holden may be tacitly if ambivalently acknowledging that, like the "mercy killer" in the film, he deserves a "life sentence." Perhaps he accepts his incarceration in California as part of that sentence.

In this context, it is tempting to remember an earlier American writer who also wrestled with the meaning of a pond in winter – a writer whom Holden does not seem to have read but whom Salinger's Buddy Glass mentions in *Seymour, An Introduction,* another work that has much to do with a dead brother. We will recall that Henry David Thoreau also lost a brother to a terrible illness and that he went to a cabin in the woods (one of Holden's recurrent fantasies) to write an implicit elegy to that brother (*A Week on the Concord and Merrimack Rivers*) and at the same time to work through complicated feelings of grief, envy, guilt, and relief.[6] Thoreau's exploration of Walden in winter perhaps finds its own encasement in the icy fishing expedition of the Eskimo in the Museum of Natural History. Both adventures, like Holden's itself, implicitly address the ambiguous sources, consequences, and significance of poems' and narratives' attempts to catch and preserve an experience that keeps sliding out of one's hand.

The problem of the pond in winter for Thoreau, of course, is not merely how one copes with death, whether it be the death of a brother or the "death" of nature or the death of one's imagination. It is in part a question of how one discovers or creates lasting values and meanings. What Thoreau discovers – or chooses to emphasize – is that the pond in winter is not "dead": like Thoreau himself, it is in "hibernation." In its frozen state, in fact, it makes possible certain kinds of exploration not possible at any other season. Thoreau can walk on it and both literally and figuratively take its measure. His exploration reveals to him that epiphanies still lurk in its depths, available to the skillful fisherman. Studying the pickerel brought to the surface, he expresses himself "always surprised by their rare beauty, as if they were fabulous fishes . . . I never chanced to see its kind in any market."[7] Such fishes, like Holden's "secret goldfish," are not for the marketplace. They are best appreciated in their own special exhibit. In fact, we can stretch a point and compare ice-covered Walden to the glass cases that Holden values for keeping precious experiences both available (to an audience) and yet safe from harm. Think of the final words that the cab driver Horwitz shouts to Holden: "Listen . . . If you was a fish, Mother Nature'd take care of *you,* wouldn't she? Right? You don't think them fish just *die* when it gets to be winter, do ya?" (109) Whether or not "Mother Nature" takes such care of fishes and birds, Holden's narrative tries implicitly to do so.

But in preserving in his narrative his "winter" experiences, both literal and metaphorical, Holden is also preserving himself. Although Holden is preoccupied at Christmas time with the problem raised by the ducks in the Central Park lagoon, Horwitz, in insisting on talking about the lagoon's fish instead, may be saying something that is equally applicable to Holden's situation:

> They live right *in* the goddam ice. It's their nature, for Chrissake. They get frozen right in one position for the whole winter. . . . Their bodies take in nutrition and all, right through the goddam seaweed and crap that's in the ice. They got their *pores* open the whole time. That's their *nature,* for Chrissake. (108)

Perhaps Holden too has survived because, during the entire winter of his discontent, he has had his "pores open the whole time," has been absorbing all of that experience – not because he has been trying consciously and systematically to absorb it, but because it's his "nature" to be both a rememberer and a narrator.

Narrating his memories thus helps Holden to deal, if imperfectly, not only with death but more generally with loss and absence. Death after all is simply one of the most striking forms of loss. Although he claims that "I never care too much when I lose something . . . I never seem to have anything that if I lost it I'd care too much" (117), he clearly does have some experiences and individuals in his past that he does worry about having lost. Being entirely alone is one of his greatest sources of pain. Even his fantasies of escaping west or to the woods involve being with *someone*. For him, loneliness and depression go hand in hand. Absence is what he most fears. His present talking to "you" is thus perhaps the verbal equivalent of his holding hands with Jane Gallagher:

> We'd get into a goddam movie or something, and right away we'd start holding hands, and we wouldn't quit till the movie was over. And without changing the position or making a big deal out of it. You never even worried, with Jane, whether your hand was sweaty or not. All you knew was, you were happy. You really were. (103)

In many respects, in fact, the "you" to whom he narrates becomes a surrogate for audiences he has lost, whether a Jane Gallagher or a dead brother. It is significant that, during his Christmas adventures, Holden resorts when alone and most depressed to an imagined listener, his brother Allie (129, 257). Eight months later, in establishing a confiding relationship with his implied narrative audience, he is dealing with the absence of Allie and even of Phoebe by creating new siblings for himself, making that audience of peers into a family.

But talking to an ideal "family" of listeners – taking the risk of putting himself on exhibit before a trustworthy audience – is not merely a way of filling the void created by the loss or absence of his own family. It is a way of coping with his own imagined absence. During his terrifying walk up Fifth Avenue, he does not pray to his dead brother to save him from dying but rather asks him repeatedly, "Allie, don't let me disappear" (257). The worst thing in the world for Holden is not the thought of dying, it is the thought of being forgotten. The solipsistic action of merely talking to himself is not enough to confirm his presence and identity. It is, to borrow the famous Zen koan with which Salinger prefaces his *Nine Stories*, like the sound of one hand clapping. It takes the presence of a listener to confirm his own presence, a listener who may remember him when he is no longer speaking and who may pass on his narrative – or at least funny, striking images of him – to yet other listeners in the "beautiful reciprocal arrangement" that Antolini calls, not "education," but "history" and "poetry" (246).

It thus seems entirely plausible that, for the seven or so hours it would take Holden to narrate his story out loud, he has not been particularly trying either to "educate" himself, to achieve some sort of therapy for himself on the basis of conscious knowledge, or to educate his listeners, whatever they may wish to infer on their own. He does not know what to think "about all this stuff I just finished telling you about," and in important respects he does not care. But, although he has not admitted as much explicitly, he has tried to "catch" and keep his listeners' attention as a way of achieving both the companionship and the witnessing of his existence that he so deeply needs. If he has put not only his experience but himself on exhibit in order to hold their interest, he has implicitly brought them into the exhibit case with him. But no one can talk forever. Conversations must finally be ended, companions part, and loss and absence appear again. When his voice ceases, and his control as uninterrupted narrator ends, Holden will disappear, unless others "miss" him enough to feel impelled to re-present him. Hence, in the final chapter, Holden tries to control the terms on which he says good-by. As he says when leaving Pencey, "I don't care if it's a sad good-by or a bad good-by, but when I leave a place I like to *know* I'm leaving it. If you don't, you feel even worse" (7). He wants to leave his audience, at the end, with that sort of memorable good-by. And he tries to do so, at least in part, by getting in the last word. As an actor in his narrative, he has tried as often as possible to have that last word. Even after Sally Hayes hangs up the phone on him, he keeps talking to her (196). Sometimes that last word has taken the form of a final defiance. Leaving Pencey, he has paused long enough to yell "at the top of my goddam voice, *Sleep tight, ya morons!*" (68). Even in his imagined death he leaves open possible room to control his own epitaph, the final word on himself:

> I think . . . if I ever die, and they stick me in a cemetery, and I have a tombstone and all, it'll say "Holden Caulfield" on it, and then what year I was born and what year I died, and then right under that it'll say "Fuck you." I'm positive in fact. (264)

There is a charming ambiguity in Holden's imagined epitaph. If the "you" refers to him, "Fuck you" represents the final indignity that society or the world can inflict upon mummies and innocent children and things Holden values. If considered as a parting shot from his own voice, however – like his final shout at Pencey – it reveals a narrator going out with not a whimper but a bang.

Holden's final words in *The Catcher in the Rye* are of course far from a defiant shout. After all, they are spoken not to a "crumby" or "phony" person but to a valued audience. Nevertheless, they embody the kind of resonant vagueness that seems intended to put the final stamp on the remembered Holden, even as the audience moves on to new narratives and new museums. Holden savors the fact that his sister "writes books all the time. Only she doesn't finish them" (89). Keeping them unfinished is analogous to keeping the Eskimo fishing in the ice or the birds flying south. In similar fashion, Holden concludes his narrative not only inconclusively but – to his audience, at least – confusingly:

> If you want to know the truth, I don't *know* what I think about [all this stuff I just finished telling you about]. I'm sorry I told so many people about it. About all I know is, I sort of *miss* everybody I told about. . . . It's funny. Don't ever tell anybody anything. If you do, you start missing everybody. (276–7)

Although some critics have wanted to treat these statements as a Zen paradox, they certainly do not constitute a paradox in the strict sense. What one *can* experience is the engaging movement of the language. Thinking "about" (that is, thinking with reference to) slides into "about all" (that is, nearly all) and on to "told about," remembering thus merging into telling. "Everybody," treated as the object of "I miss," gives way to "anybody" as the indirect object of "tell," then returns as the object of "you start missing," as "I" makes way for "you." Perhaps Holden is using his final words to offer psychological or religious insights, but those insights are veiled or blurred at best. What his words do offer, if nothing else, is the dance of his language itself, the hum and buzz, as Whitman would say, of his "valvéd voice." Like the ending, Holden's narrative as a whole constitutes a tonally various "song of myself" that, just as the young boy's singing of "Coming through the Rye" gets taken up by Holden, may in turn get caught and carried on by Holden's listeners, simply for the pleasures of the singing if not for its elusive lessons.

In the confusing pains and pleasures of the remembered song, his audience, Holden may hope, will "miss" and "tell" him. There may be something finally mischievous and even competitive in this, both on Holden's part and on the part of his creator. We know that he likes to "horse around," even with those like Jane and Phoebe whom he most cares about. It is thus tempting, as part of an audience's memory of Holden, to remember one of his earlier comments: "All you have to do is say something nobody understands and they'll do practically anything you want them to" (205).

## NOTES

1. J. D. Salinger, *The Catcher in the Rye* (Boston: Little, Brown, 1951), p. 158. Subsequent parenthetical references are to this edition.
2. The role of modern ethnographic museums in turning cultural processes and products into aesthetic objects and in creating cultural narratives that privilege and rationalize the power of the collectors is provocatively explored in George W. Stocking, Jr., *Objects and Others: Essays on Museums and Material Culture* (Madison: University of Wisconsin Press, 1985).
3. Salinger's use of a narrating character must, of course, confront the kinds of technical difficulties other authors have had to face in using this convention. Without belaboring these difficulties, it may be useful to recount them briefly, since some of them also bear on the novel's thematic problematics. For example, Salinger needs the reader to trust the basic reliability of Holden's representation of the facts of the narrative – to trust his insistent "I really did," "I really wouldn't," "he really was," and so forth as consistent with his assertion, as he says of D. B., that writers should only write about what they really know something about (212). In fact, Salinger must periodically strain our sense of verisimilitude in order to use Holden's narrative as a conduit for material Salinger considers it essential for us to confront – think, for example, of Holden's verbatim reporting of Antolini's long and elaborate speech, which he supposedly hears while dead tired and

"dizzy" (242–7). Salinger tries to soften this convention by allowing Holden a faulty memory at points where it won't harm the narrative; for example, he swears several times that "I can't remember" many of the details of his fight with Stradlater over Jane Gallagher (52–7), but that doesn't at all prevent us from grasping the drama of, or Holden's motives for, the fight. Salinger not only intends Holden's occasional factual inaccuracies to be obvious to most readers, but he uses most of those inaccuracies to make him more endearing as a character – as when he reports his claim to Sunny that he's just had an operation on his "clavichord" (126) – or to advance our understanding of his character as when he holds on, despite Phoebe's correction, to the phrase "catch a body" (224). (Holden retrospectively acknowledges, in what Salinger seems to intend as a revealing acknowledgment, that the correct phrase is "meet a body.")

4. Nathaniel Hawthorne, *The Scarlet Letter* (Columbus: Ohio State University Press, 1962), p. 4.
5. Numerous critics operate explicitly or implicitly on the assumption that Holden is in some sort of psychiatric facility, and often base key elements of their interpretations on the assumption that he has suffered and may (many argue) be finally recovering from an emotional breakdown or existential crisis. A few critics see the institution as simply some sort of hospital or rest home and stress his breakdown as more physical than psychological. The evidence that Holden himself offers does not conclusively resolve this disagreement. But I believe Warren French is essentially correct in his commonsense stressing of the role of Holden's poor physical condition at Christmas in leading to and intensifying his "breakdown." Certainly many of Holden's physical symptoms during his frenetic to-and-fro in Manhattan – his constant dizziness, fainting spells, and nausea – seem at least as much the product of lack of sleep and food and too much drinking as they do of his admittedly serious depression.
6. See Salinger, *Raise High the Roof Beam, Carpenters and Seymour, An Introduction* (Boston: Little, Brown, 1959), p. 161. The complex emotional and imaginative relationship that Henry Thoreau had with his brother John, who died painfully of lockjaw in 1842, is recounted in persuasive detail in Richard Lebeaux, *Young Man Thoreau* (Amherst: University of Massachusetts Press, 1977), especially chapter 6.
7. Henry David Thoreau, *Walden*, ed. Jay Lyndon Shanley (Princeton, N.J.: Princeton University Press, 1971), pp. 284–5.

4

# Pencey Preppy: Cultural Codes in *The Catcher in the Rye*

CHRISTOPHER BROOKEMAN

HOLDEN Caulfield, like Huck Finn, has become a mythic figure of adolescent rebellion in American culture. One continuing rich source for this presentation of Holden, usually as a rebel against the conformist pressures of post–Second World War American society, is the American history textbook designed for high school use. In a typical example, Daniel F. Davis and Norman Langer, authors of *A History of the United States Since 1945*, argue that Holden's "adventures say a great deal about the worth of the individual in American society. They also remind readers how vulnerable every individual can be."[1] This analysis forms part of a chapter in their textbook entitled "Literature: The Individual and Society," in which the conformist society against which Holden rebels is constructed out of a number of sociological studies of the American character published at about the same time as *The Catcher in the Rye*. One book of this type, David Riesman's *The Lonely Crowd* (1950), provides their descriptive model of the ideology of modern American society against which Holden is seen as making an individualistic stand. They paraphrase Riesman as follows:

> As societies become more technologically advanced, Riesman argued, parents give up some of their authority to other institutions such as schools, the mass media, and peer groups. . . . Riesman called this new society "other-directed." Riesman maintained that

I would like to thank Amy Gadney, who was the teenage consultant; Rupert Wilkinson, Ralph Willett, and Tony Dunn, ex-teenagers who read various drafts with helpful suggestions; and the 1988 graduates in English at the Polytechnic of Central London, who kept me on my theoretical toes. Thanks also to P.C.L. Languages Library and their computer search facilities.

> other-directed societies lead to stability and tolerance, but also foster conformity and loss of individuality. He illustrated the point by telling the story of a boy who, when asked if he would like to fly replied, "I would like to be able to fly if everyone else did."[2]

This cult status of Holden as a generalized champion of American individualism and indicator of the psychic disturbances caused by the stresses of postindustrial society is evident not only in the world of high school textbooks. In a book by the cultural critic Christopher Lasch, *Haven in a Heartless World: The Family Besieged* (1977), we find the following assessment of the seminal status of Holden as a weathervane for the various anxieties that have developed within the nuclear family as parental authority has declined in modern America:

> Films, comic strips, and popular novels – in particular the many novels of adolescent revolt, patterned after J. D. Salinger's "The Catcher in the Rye" – ridicule the 'manifest' father, and authority in general, while depicting 'latent' father-figures as sinister, aggressive, and utterly unprincipled in their persecution of their hero or heroine.[3]

By turning Holden into a symptom of a general cultural malaise, critics have failed to give attention to the fact that Salinger locates Holden's story within a very specific social world in which the most significant influence is not some generalized concept of American culture or society, but the codes and practices of a particular instrument of social control – the American prep school. Even when the action moves to New York, Holden stays, in the main, within a finely tuned collegiate culture of dates and moviegoing. This is clear from his description of the sociology of the clientele in a Greenwich Village nightclub named after the resident pianist: "Even though it was so late, old Ernie's was jam-packed, mostly with prep school jerks and college jerks."[4] It is within the immediate, primary context of Pencey Prep, where we first encounter Holden, that we need to situate all the agencies that seek to influence his development, such as the peer group, parents, and the mass media. Only then will we do justice to J. D. Salinger's portrait of the anxiety-ridden adolescent within the particular fraction of the middle class whose behavior and psychology are the substance of *The Catcher in the Rye.*

Holden seems to have attended three prep schools: Whooton, Elkton Hills, and Pencey. The character and function of this type of private school is delineated in David Riesman's portrait of such a school in the late 1940s, taken from his companion book to *The Lonely Crowd*, called *Faces in the Crowd* (1952):

> Livingston School, a boys' preparatory school in a small Connecticut town, draws on the top of the social system . . . from the East. . . . Its masters are mostly graduates of Ivy League colleges. . . . It is not as old a school as St. Marks . . . or as civilized as Choate . . . [the masters] look askance at innovation.[5]

The evolution of single-sex boarding schools like St. Mark's and Choate (which John F. Kennedy attended) had a specific function which Holden experiences. In its purest form this kind of school was created in the nineteenth century to educate, socialize, and monitor the male offspring of the professional and business classes. As modern society developed its diverse industrial and administrative systems, such institutions as the church, the ancient universities, and the family began to cede power and responsibility for educating and controlling children to others. Throughout the nineteenth and twentieth centuries the dominant role of the family has been steadily supplanted, though not entirely replaced, by a whole range of institutions such as the school, the college, the firm, and the state bureaucracies. These institutions became places where the young future professionals of the middle and upper classes experienced an extended period of training and socialization.

An early model of this type of training institution can be derived from a letter written home to his father in Jamaica, Long Island, by the youthful Sam Ward in 1826. Sam describes his reactions to his first days at Round Hill boarding school, founded in Massachusetts in 1823 by Joseph Cogswell and George Bancroft to offer education and training to the male children of the well-to-do:

> When I came here I was pleased with the novelty of it. . . . I never had before joined with so large a number of boys. . . . I have never been in the same community, in the same fellowship and family with so many. I did not know anything scarcely of boys' customs, games, and plays, then or at most, not one quarter so much as I do now.[6]

In the interests of national leadership training, Sam has been transported from his New York home – parents, grandparents, aunts, uncles, servants black and white – to a reductive world composed of his peers and the faculty of Round Hill. The use of school uniforms in such institutions was a further symbol of this deliberate isolation of the middle-class child from the surrounding society.

What particularly strikes Sam as a new experience is the extent and depth of the culture of his peer group, which though drawn from the well-to-do of the whole nation – from New Orleans in the South to Boston in the North – is blended into homogeneity by Round Hill. The school fits them with a behavioral uniform signifying to the world the social group to which they belong or aspire to belong. The type that such schools were created to produce was the bourgeois Christian gentleman, preferably with muscles. The trustees' announcement of the goals of Groton, a prep school opened in 1884, captures the essentials of the species: "Every endeavour will be made to cultivate manly, christian character, having regard to moral and physical as well as intellectual development."[7] Holden, a post–Second World War version of Sam Ward, is deeply skeptical about this whole process of character formation supposedly carried out by such schools. The promotional material for Pencey Prep includes the statement, "Since 1888 we have been moulding boys into splendid and clear-thinking young men"(2). Holden dismisses this claim with a characteristic put-down: "Strictly for the birds." Putting Holden's views aside, it was this belief in character formation that motivated American society to initiate such institutions as Pencey Prep, and in a sense *The Catcher in the Rye,* like Sam Ward's letter to his father on Long Island, is a report home. Salinger himself attended a military version of the American prep school and must have drawn on his experiences there in writing *The Catcher in the Rye.*

Salinger employs two main ways of creating his portrait of the culture of the Eastern prep school as exemplified by the fictional Pencey of Agerstown, Pennsylvania. First there are Holden's invariably debunking assessments of prep school traditions and customs such as the one just quoted. Second there are his extended ritualistic encounters, usually with particular members of his peer group such as Ackley or Stradlater, but also with members of the faculty like Spencer, Holden's history teacher at Pencey. These encounters have the character of rituals in that they are repetitive, like exercises or verbal push-ups. They are Holden's way of keeping in shape. The form of these encounters is usually dialogue, interspersed with personal commentary by Holden.

Holden's commentaries on the value of the system of Pencey Prep lead him to conclude that the whole official vision of the school as a cooperative caring family is a mask for an actual ideology of intense competitive struggle between its individual members and factions. This official image of the prep school as an idealized family standing in loco parentis was a favorite metaphor within the historical culture and discourse of the prep school idea. Here is a biographer of Endicott Peabody, the founder of the Groton School (where Franklin Roosevelt was a pupil), describing the familial glow that irradiated from its founder:

> Therefore it was the most natural thing in the world for him to think of his school as being simply a large family. . . . [Mr. and Mrs. Peabody] said good-night to every boy in the school every night when they were there. There was an intimacy at the heart of things that was peculiar to the genius of the place.[8]

Here, by way of contrast, is Holden's considered opinion of the ideology of the Pencey system as he describes it to his date Sally Hayes:

> You ought to go to a boy's school sometime. . . . everybody sticks together in these dirty little goddam cliques. . . . Even the guys that belong to the goddam Book-of-the-Month Club stick together. (131)

Alongside the image of the family, the prep school promoted the metaphor of life as a game conducted according to the rules of fair play. Dr. Thurmer, the headmaster of Pencey, in his farewell address to Holden when he informs him that he is being thrown out for flunking four subjects and not applying himself, uses the occasion to impress on Holden that life is a "game" and "you should play it according to the rules." Holden's response, delivered to the reader, is characteristic:

> Game, my ass. Some game. If you get on the side where all the hot-shots are, then it's a game; all right – I'll admit that. But if you get on the other side . . . then what's a game about it? (8)

Holden's career in the world of team games is limited to that of being manager of the Pencey fencing team. The management of people is a key skill in postindustrial America, and Holden signally fails in this area. He loses the team foils and equipment on the subway and is consequently ostracized by the team. However, it would be wrong to see Holden as without sporting skills. He does describe himself as "a very good golfer," good enough to be asked to appear in a golfing movie short. But his personal code and hatred of the Hollywood star system, which seeks to turn all skills into commodities, makes him reject this opportunity to star. Holden turns his back on one of the greatest honors America can offer its citizens, a starring role:

> I almost was once in a movie short, but I changed my mind at the last minute. I figured that anybody that hates the movies as much as I do, I'd be a phony if I let them stick me in a movie short.(77)

Holden's ability to expose and deconstruct the contradictions within the official ideology of Pencey Prep in virtuoso asides, like some latter-day Hamlet, should not blind us to the fact that Holden is also a connoisseur and exploiter of the system he despises. He is both insider and outsider. Although he has a fantasy of fleeing from civilization like Huck Finn and living in Nature, he is very much the college man-about-town, adept at telephone dating techniques, habitué of nightclubs and hotel lounges, and possessed of that crucial urban skill of riling cab drivers. Admittedly he experiences some spectacular failures, as in the encounter with the prostitute and her pimp, but overall, the sixteen-year-old, six-foot, two-inch teenager with a crew cut and red hunting cap cannot be characterized as the eternal gauche outsider. His ability to fathom the mind-sets of his peer group gives him a radar-like awareness of social and psychological messages, often to the point of paralyzing overload. In many ways the burgeoning myth of Holden the sullen outsider obscures the degree to which he is also very gregarious and manipulative. Holden needs other people in order to define himself. He is endlessly in pursuit of company, calling people on the phone, both acquaintances and strangers, and waylaying his colleagues at Pencey as they are washing or dressing.

Viewed from this perspective, Holden's ritualistic encounters with his peer group are not just bull sessions or adolescent horseplay, but part of Salinger's extremely shrewd contribution to the considerable postwar debate on what was called the changing American social character. The era of *The Catcher in the Rye* witnessed the arrival of the sociological best seller with such books as *The Lonely Crowd* and William Whyte's *The Organization Man* (1956). A recent book that reviewed this modc of inquiry characterized it as "a national tradition, supporting an august industry of books and articles."[9] The sociologists who addressed the issue of social character as it presented itself in the 1950s were concerned with a number of themes that relate directly to Salinger's portrait of the educational culture and leisure pursuits of American middle-class adolescents. First, did Americans display a particular national identity, a set of observable common characteristics? Were Americans team players, for example, or a collection of self-reliant individualists? Second, what agencies performed the process of socialization and what techniques were used? This second theme usually led to discussions of which agencies among the various that were active in modern society were the most influential: the family, the peer group, the mass and so forth. Holden's running commentary on society is an index of his negotiations with these various agencies, which is probably why the book has a cult status among teenagers. It has the quality of a training manual on techniques of survival.

A particular emphasis within this genre of the sociological study of American character was a concern with the role of leisure in modern mass society: America at play, or in Holden's definition, "horsing around." Holden seems to exist in a world almost entirely composed of leisure pursuits. We hardly ever see him in a context of anything that might be called work, which in his case would be academic study. His usual milieu is one in which he is socializing with a member or members of his peer group. Salinger makes his hero self-conscious about this trait: "Sometimes I horse around quite a lot, just to keep from getting bored"(21).

The nineteenth-century promoters of the virtues of the prep

school were very worried about this kind of peer group horseplay, which seems to be a social grist, basic to life at Pencey. Here is the Reverend Endicott Peabody warning against the dangers of the kind of peer group interaction that is a daily ritual for Holden and "old Ackley":

> It seems to me of the utmost importance that there should be nothing of the nature of loafing in a school. The curse of American college life and of school life is loafing. Boys and men get together in a sociable way and sit around a room and talk and gossip, and a little scandal comes in, and then evil. The tone of loafers is always low.[10]

What Salinger shows is a world in which the loafing habits of teenagers, the peer group and its culture, have become a way of life; and although Salinger does not directly moralize about his hero's condition, there is something tragic about the sadly contracted state of Holden's world from which other generations have withdrawn, leaving his own generation to its one-dimensional fate.

In the postwar debate on American social character, everyone seemed to agree that peer group pressure and autonomy had reached alarming proportions. A typical example of the prose style employed and the conclusions reached by this growth industry of studies into the condition of America's youth can be seen in a 1973 publication entitled *Youth: Transition to Adulthood, Report of the Panel on Youth of the President's Science Advisory Committee,* which gives the following assessment of the marooned status of Holden and his fellows within modern America:

> Youth are segregated from adults by the economic and educational institutions created by adults; they are deprived of psychic support from persons of other ages, a psychic support that once came from the family; they are subordinate and powerless in relation to adults, and outsiders to the dominant social institutions. Yet they have money, they have access to a wide range of communications media, and control of some, and they are relatively large in number. All these elements combine to create the special characteristics of the youth culture.[11]

The single book that established this genre of study, its language and diagnostic content, was Riesman's *The Lonely Crowd: A Study of the Changing American Character.* Within the book are a cluster of perceptions on the process of socialization and the role of the peer group that can serve as a guide and a point of departure for an analysis of the role of these factors in *The Catcher in the Rye.*

Riesman's discussion of the role of the peer group as a socializing instrument is generated out of an historical model of how individuals have been socialized at different times in Western society. It is therefore important to place the book in this general theoretical context. In his preface Riesman suggests that social influence should and can be positive and supportive, and is probably essential:

> In order that any society may function well, its members must acquire the kind of character which makes them want to act in the way that they have to act as members of the society or of a special class within it.[12]

This optimistic reading of the impact of society on the individual, the notion of a beneficial social character, is derived from the neo-Freudian theoretician Erich Fromm, with whom Riesman had studied. Fromm attempted to revise Freud's pessimistic reading of the way civilization restricts and curbs individual freedom. He constructed a model of personal development which directed attention away from the traumas of childhood toward a belief that external agencies of socialization, like the school, could have a creative influence on the development of the individual. A view emerged within the Frommian school that the healthy growth of the human personality is dependent upon membership in the social group. The child that grows to maturity outside a social group becomes an animal, without language, knowledge, the capacity to reason, or the ability to love.

A contradiction emerges in Riesman's actual findings, however, and in critical reception to his book. There is a suggestion that the agencies he described as mediating social character in a postindustrial world, such as the corporation and the mass media, were themselves alarmingly repressive and were creating an aimless lonely crowd of atomized, alienated, anxious Americans. Riesman's model is founded on a paradox. He wishes to preserve and promote the classic liberal demands of personal freedom and diversity, but he draws back from an idea of complete individual autonomy. Riesman attaches great value to the importance of a social character that should be internalized by the individual: "It is one of the ambiguities of human existence, as it is of art, that personal life flourishes within the forms provided for it by tradition and necessity."[13] This in brief is the theoretical context for Riesman's researches into the actual behavior of modern Americans. This theoretical model must in turn be placed within the historical sequence of the emergence of the three models of how the individual and a specific social character interact.

Riesman's first model describes how belief is organized in feudal society. In feudal society all values are communal, so there is no need for a concept of the individual: "ritual, routine, and religion serve to occupy and orient everyone."[14] This form of social character is called "tradition-directed" and operates like a form of osmosis. Tradition-directed medieval society then gives way during the Renaissance to a new individualistic ideology of bourgeois capitalism. In order to take advantage of the new market society, the idea of the entrepreneurial self develops. No longer tradition-directed, people become inner-directed; parents must now implant in their offspring a new psychological mechanism appropriate to a more open society. Riesman calls this device a gyroscope which will enable the inner-directed individual "to receive and utilize certain signals from the outside, provided that they can be reconciled with the limited maneuverability that his gyroscope permits him. His pilot is not quite automatic."[15]

The main psychological difference between a tradition-directed society and an inner-directed one is that the former implants its values through shame, while the latter internalizes its values through guilt and conscience. A classic example of the way an inner-directed society internalizes its values is the scene in *Little Women* (1868) in which the March children learn the notion of deferred gratification, a crucial lesson for the nineteenth-century middle-class child. It is also instructive to compare the latter's portrait of adolescence with that of *The Catcher in the Rye.* On Christmas Day the March family, with the father absent at the Civil War, is about to enjoy a far from luxurious breakfast when Mrs. March makes an appeal to her four daughters:

> Merry Christmas little daughters! I'm glad you began at once, and hope you will keep on. But I want to say one word before we sit down. Not far from here lies a poor woman with a little new-born baby. Six children are huddled into one bed to keep from freezing, for they have no fire. There is nothing to eat over there; and the oldest boy came to tell me they were suffering hunger and cold. My girls, will you give them your breakfast as a Christmas present?[16]

Riesman's assessment of the shift from a feudal society to a capitalist one of deferred gratification is based on the performance of upwardly mobile elites. He continues this perspective when he comes to his third social character, the other-directed type which can be observed in the culture of a particular socioeconomic group that emerged as a distinct segment in postwar America. Riesman identifies this group as belonging to "the upper middle class of our larger cities: more prominent in Los Angeles than in Spokane, in Cincinnati than in Chillicothe."[17] Riesman's term "other-directed" marks a shift from an industrial society, where manufacturing is the engine room of the economy and culture, to a postindustrial economy where the service sector is more important than the manufacturing sector. This postindustrial world of leisure industries, financial services, and consumption rather than production is the world of *The Catcher in the Rye.* Holden's absent father is a corporation lawyer and investor in Broadway shows, and his brother D. B. is a script writer in Hollywood. The novel's economic base is invariably postindustrial. A classic example of this kind of economic activity, in which people make money from providing services rather than goods, can be seen in Holden's description of a recent benefactor of Pencey Prep, which as an educational institution is itself part of the service sector of the economy:

> When I lived at Pencey, I lived in the Ossenburger Memorial Wing of the new dorms. . . . It was named after this guy Ossenburger that went to Pencey. He made a pot of dough in the undertaking business after he got out of Pencey. (16)

Other firm indicators of the arrival of the postindustrial culture in *Catcher in the Rye* are the dominance of the peer group, the pervasive influence of the mass media, and the decline of parental authority.

One literary sign that Salinger is conscious of the waning of the inner-directed individual is his conscious parody, at the beginning of *The Catcher in the Rye,* of the classic cultural form of an inner-directed culture, the realistic novel of the nineteenth century in which developmental individuals move through chronological time from cradle to grave. Here is Salinger's postmodernist opening:

> If you really want to hear about it, the first thing you probably want to know is where I was born, and what my lousy childhood was. . . . all that David Copperfield kind of crap . . . (1)

Salinger makes his hero refuse the reader this kind of biographical information, which Holden finds boring and irrelevant and too "personal." Salinger's postmodernist unease with the culture and literature of inner-direction is based on a perception that American society, at the middle-class level, is no longer operating through rugged individualism although vestiges of the old ideology remain. This idea that society is often in a state of transition between two social characters is present in Riesman's thinking as well. Here is Riesman on the contradictions faced by the prep school student in postwar America:

> Another location where we might expect to find inner-direction in fairly aboriginal form is a conservative New England prep school for boys where the elderly seek to control along traditional lines the training and values of youth. . . . the characterological struggle (between inner and other-direction) is carried out inside them.[18]

Holden is caught in just such a struggle for his identity, as inner-directed agencies like Pencey compete for his soul with other-directed ones like the mass media.

There are further contradictions, particularly if one tries to apply Riesman's linear grid to other Western societies. In an essay on the interactions between American and Italian popular music in the postwar era, Alessandro Portelli has pointed out the importance of taking into account local factors when applying Riesman:

> David Riesman has pointed out how changes in patterns of musical consumption were an aspect of the shift from an "inner-directed" to an "other-directed" type in national character. If we apply his model to Italy, we find that the change was much sharper. In fact,

> post-war Italy may be said to have moved from "tradition-directed" to "other-directed" without really experiencing the "inner-directed" stage at all. Industrialization, emigration, urbanization, the increase of schooling and mass communication, the availability of foreign examples, all these eroded the traditional and reassuring authority of the Church and family (and of the totalitarian state).[19]

Despite these caveats, Holden Caulfield is clearly well on his way toward being entirely formed by a postindustrial, other-directed culture, particularly in the stress he lays on the values of his peer group as he tries to win their approval. Riesman saw that the main role of the peer group was to train young people in the art of sociability, which is a key skill in postindustrial America, where the art of public relations and the manipulation of people are highly prized attributes. These skills are necessary for the professional managers of people who must combine enough "technical knowledge to talk to the technical men with enough social skills to sense the wants of the variety of publics that may affect or be affected by their decisions."[20]

Holden is endlessly called upon to perform in this way – to sense other people's needs, to negotiate his way into and out of interpersonal situations with teachers, fellow students, cab drivers, brothers and sisters. What Salinger shows through Holden is someone cracking up and breaking down under the pressure of a society in which social leisure and communication have become full-time occupations. The culture of the adolescent has been invaded by the needs of personnel management and diplomacy. An enormous amount of Holden's time and energy is spent trying, with varying degrees of success, to relate to people, usually by means of elaborate courtship-like rituals through which another person's worldview is sniffed out. A classic instance of this process is Holden's anecdote about Dick Slagle's suitcases.

While he was at Elkton Hills, Holden had roomed with a student named Dick Slagle. Dick Slagle is embarrassed by the cheapness of his suitcases, particularly as Holden's parents have fitted him out with "genuine cowhide" ones from Mark Cross. Holden, realizing that his roommate has an inferiority complex about his cheap cases, tries to protect Dick's feelings by hiding his cowhide suitcases under the bed, only to discover that Dick has taken them out and is pretending that they are really his. Poor Slagle is not content with this single strategy; he faces both ways on the issue by also attacking Holden's taste:

> He was always saying snotty things about them, my suitcases, for instance. He kept saying they were too new and bourgeois. That was his favourite goddam word. . . . Even my fountain pen was bourgeois. (108)

The main emotion released by these repetitive encounters in which codes and values are clarified is status anxiety, the desire to become invisible beyond comment within a group, and therefore to have your membership in the group confirmed. There does not seem to be much room for marginal differentiation. This incident of the suitcases could easily have appeared as a case study to illustrate Riesman's theories of other-direction. Instead of the metaphor of the gyroscope, which orients the individual to society's values in an inner-directed society, Riesman argues that the new middle-class person in an other-directed society scans the culture by means of "radar," seeking for the reference points that explain how to negotiate the terrain of the post-industrial world. Blips and mistakes in cultural navigation are identified and relayed to the individual on his or her radar screen: "As against guilt-and-shame controls, though of course these survive, one prime psychological lever of the other-directed person is a diffuse anxiety."[21] A good example of the climate of anxiety and fear in which Holden exists, and in which the antennae of his radar have to be continually alert to detect other people's identities, values, and probings, is his story about Louis Gorman. Louis was a fellow student of Holden's at Whooton School and the incident is another example of what we might call the right suitcase syndrome. While in the middle of what he thought was a normal conversation about tennis with Louis, Louis suddenly asks Holden if he happened to know where the Catholic church was. Holden realizes that all the time Louis was really probing Holden to find out whether he was a Catholic. Holden's reaction to this event is instructive: "That kind of stuff drives me crazy. . . . It's just like those suitcases I was telling you about, in a way."(113)

Alongside the peer group and directly related to its operations are the mass media. Riesman's description of this relationship is as follows:

> The peer group accepts a substantial responsibility in the flow of modern communications. It stands midway between the individuals of whom each group is composed and the messages which flow to the group's opinion leaders from the mass media. The mass media are the wholesalers; the peer groups, the retailers of the communications industry.[22]

The main focus for Holden and the mass media are Hollywood films. It is a love-hate relationship; Hollywood values are basically "phony," though they are an important source of discriminations and reference points which Holden and his peer group retail to one another. The main way such judgments are circulated is by the use of a specialized discourse, a technique that Riesman describes as follows:

> All "knobby" or idiosyncratic qualities are more or less eliminated or repressed. And judgements of others by peer group members are so clearly matters of taste that their expression has to resort to the vaguest phrases, constantly changed: cute, lousy, square, darling, good guy, honey, swell, bitch (without precise meaning), etc.[23]

A Holden Caulfield version of this discourse would include the following: "phony," "and all," "goddam," "flitty," "joe-Yale," and an expression that Holden feels he has to explain to the reader, "give him a locomotive – that's a cheer."

A particular aspect of Salinger's treatment of the peer group and its activities is the way Holden's brothers, D. B. and Allie, and his younger sister Phoebe are more like members of his peer group than of his family. Holden is fascinated by the codes and values of the world of his younger sister, into which he virtually retreats toward the end of his lost weekend in New York. He also holds long imaginary conversations with his revered dead brother Allie. His relationship with his older brother D. B. is complicated by Holden's feeling that D. B. has "prostituted" himself by working in Hollywood, though they clearly were close. It was D. B. who introduced Holden to Ernie's, the nightclub in Greenwich Village. This closeness to his brothers and sister is in stark contrast to the relation with his parents, who are absent, shadowy figures. In a conversation on the train to New York with Mrs. Morrow, the mother of a fellow student at Pencey, Holden silently concludes that "All mothers are slightly insane." To complete the portrait of the modern family Holden has this fairly original relationship with his grandmother:

> I have this grandmother that's pretty lavish with her dough. She doesn't have all her marbles any more – she's as old as hell – and she keeps sending me money for my birthday about four times a year. (52)

Although the dominant agency of social control in Holden's world is the peer group, which in Riesman's chronology has replaced such formerly powerful agencies as family, governess, and educational institution, the mass media in the shape of Hollywood movies are also crucial to Holden's worldview. He conceives the relationship as follows:

> I hate the movies like poison, but I get a bang imitating them . . . "I'm the goddam Governor's son. . . . He doesn't want me to be a tap dancer. He wants me to go to Oxford." (29)

The particular film that Holden loathes but can't stop imitating is M.G.M.'s 1946 musical *Ziegfeld Follies* starring Fred Astaire and Lucille Ball, directed by Vincente Minnelli. Holden's stand against the stars, styles, and emotional conventions of Hollywood is a losing one insofar as the collegiate culture on which he is socially dependent has since the 1920s elevated the culture of Hollywood to central status. Holden's dates often include a visit to a movie, which is then discussed in detail in order to establish its status within the canon. Holden's sister Phoebe has an obsession with *The Thirty-Nine Steps* (1935) starring Robert Donat: "She knows the whole goddam movie by heart, because I've taken her to see it about ten times" (67). What Hollywood movies provide for Holden and his peers are definitions of manners and of emotional and psychological conventions. The appearance of *The Catcher in the Rye* coincided with a continuing national debate about the role of mass culture that was a distinctive feature of intellectual life in postwar America.[24] Sometimes Holden comes on like F. R. Leavis or T. S. Eliot, talking about "phony" false consciousness and manipulation; but he also displays a (admittedly somewhat begrudging) postmodernist delight in the iconography and conventions of mass cultural formulas. An example of Holden in his negative mode is his critique of a film that seems to be a composite of several films, one of a cycle in which Hollywood explored the idea of amnesia. It is probably *Random Harvest* (1942), starring Ronald Colman and Greer Garson. Holden's comment on the film is as follows: "All I can say is, don't see it if you don't want to puke all over yourself"(139). James Agee's review was a little more subtle:

> I would like to recommend this film to those who can stay interested in Ronald Colman's amnesia for two hours and who could with pleasure eat a bowl of Yardley's shaving cream for breakfast.[25]

Holden seems to be a vehicle for Salinger's own views of Hollywood, which are as contradictory and detailed as Holden's. Ian Hamilton's controversial and extremely sketchy biography of Salinger reports that:

> Salinger himself, it is evident, from early on had a fan's encyclopedic grasp of cine lore. To this day, his favourite home entertainment (we've been told) is playing old films from the 1940's, of which he has a connoisseur's collection.[26]

In 1948, when *The Catcher in the Rye* was a work in progress, Lionel Trilling gave this report on the state of the contemporary American novel:

> So far as the novel touches social and political questions it permits itself to choose only between a cheery or a sour democratism; it is questionable whether any American novel since *Babbitt* has told us a new thing about our social life. In psychology the novel relies either on a mechanical or a clinical use of psychiatry or on the insights that were established by the novelists of fifty years ago.[27]

By Trilling's criteria *The Catcher in the Rye* does not break radically new ground, though it is clear, in my view, that Holden is an extremely shrewd indicator of the emerging postindustrial society. But there are also some very strong literary influences in the book that seem to shape Salinger's imagination. The world of preppy collegiate manners, peer groups, endless socializing and consumption is not a new one in American culture. It is a world first and most famously associated with F. Scott Fitzgerald. Holden is "crazy about 'The Great Gatsby' " and Salinger directly signals this kind of intertextuality when he names one of the characters in *The Catcher in the Rye* "Bernice something – Crabs or Krebs"(73). In this one jumbled name Salinger alludes both to a short story by Fitzgerald called "Bernice Bobs Her Hair" and to one by Hemingway called "Soldier's Home," in which a young soldier named Krebs comes back late from the First World War and tries to adapt to the world of small-town America. What is particularly interesting about the Hemingway story as a source for Salinger is that one of the few people to whom Krebs can relate is his younger sister, who is something of a junior baseball star and refers to her brother as her "beau." Like Holden, Krebs is drawn to the world of the preadolescent child.

Further evidence for the strong presence of 1920s literary culture as a model for Salinger is provided by Paula Fass in her book *The Damned and the Beautiful: American Youth in the 1920's.* Fass clearly shows that the one-dimensional world that Holden inherits was already in place by the twenties. Her researches are based on the same social group as we find in Salinger, a group she identifies as follows: "One major segment of the youth population – native, white, middle-class, and almost exclusively college going."[28] Just two of her observations will suffice to show how structural and complete was the historical arrival of this youth culture to a position of relative autonomy by the 1920s. First, Fass cites a study of car use that revealed that "more than 40% of one sample of California high-school boys had the use of the family car whenever they wished, and almost one quarter owned their own car."[29] She concludes that "it can be safely assumed that most of the free afternoons and evenings were spent by the young with their peers."[30] Second, Fass notes data directly relevant to the theme of Holden's moviegoing:

> Most students regularly attended one movie per week, and students were especially interested in the personalities, tastes, and interests of movie stars who were given full coverage in columns, reviews, and interviews.[31]

In many ways *The Catcher in the Rye* is a finely tuned linguistic and cultural updating of the collegiate tales of F. Scott Fitzgerald, a shrewd portrait of a particular youth subculture within a specific socioeconomic and class fraction of American society. If Trilling had been able to include the novel in his 1948 round-up, he would not have been so gloomy about the state of the modern American novel.

## NOTES

1. Daniel F. Davis and Norman Langer, *A History of the United States since 1945* (New York: Scholastic, 1987), p. 71.
2. Ibid., p. 70. For the record, Riesman's American Icarus is actually a girl.
3. Christopher Lasch, *Haven in a Heartless World: The Family Besieged* (New York: Basic Books, 1979), p. 176.
4. J. D. Salinger, *The Catcher in the Rye* (New York: Bantam, 1964), p. 83. All subsequent page references, appearing in parentheses in the text, are to this edition.
5. David Riesman, *Faces in the Crowd* (New Haven: Yale University Press, 1952), p. 282.
6. Samuel Ward III to Samuel Ward II, August 1st, 1826, Ward Family MSS. For this illustration and several others I am indebted to James McLachlan, *American Boarding Schools* (New York: Scribner's, 1970).
7. Frank D. Ashburn, *Peabody of Groton: A Portrait* (New York, 1914), p. 68.
8. Ibid., p. 71.
9. Rupert Wilkinson, *The Pursuit of American Character* (New York: Harper and Row, 1988), p. 1.
10. Endicott Peabody, "The Continuous Moral Influence of the School through College and Life," *School Review* 7 (1899): 627–28.
11. *Youth: Transition to Adulthood, Report of the Panel on Youth of the President's Science Advisory Committee* (Washington, D.C.: U.S. Government Printing Office, 1973), p. 125.
12. David Riesman, *The Lonely Crowd: A Study of the Changing American Character* (New Haven: Yale University Press, rev. ed. 1970), p. 5.
13. Ibid., pp. 5–6.
14. Ibid., p. 11.
15. Ibid., pp. 16–17.
16. Louisa M. Alcott, *Little Women* (London: J. M. Dent, 1948), p. 18.
17. Riesman, *The Lonely Crowd,* p. 19.
18. Riesman, *Faces in the Crowd,* p. 272.

19. Alessandro Portelli, "The Paper Tiger and the Teddy Bear," in *Cultural Change in the United States since World War II,* ed. Christopher W. E. Bigsby et al. (Amsterdam: Free University Press, 1986), p. 84.
20. Riesman, *The Lonely Crowd,* p. 135.
21. Ibid., p. 26.
22. Ibid., p. 85.
23. Ibid., p. 71.
24. For a summary of these issues see C. E. Brookeman, *American Culture and Society since the 1930's* (London: Macmillan, 1984).
25. Agee's comment can be found in Leslie Halliwell, *Halliwell's Film Guide,* 5th ed. (London: Grafton Books, 1986), p. 803. I am indebted to Ed Buscombe and his fellow buffs at the British Film Institute for hunting down these film references.
26. Ian Hamilton, *In Search of J. D. Salinger* (New York: Random House, 1988), pp. 106–7.
27. Lionel Trilling, *The Liberal Imagination* (Oxford: Oxford University Press, 1980), p. 249.
28. Paula S. Fass, *The Damned and the Beautiful: American Youth in the 1920's* (Oxford: Oxford University Press, 1979), p. 7.
29. Ibid., p. 218.
30. Ibid., p. 217.
31. Ibid., pp. 206–7.

5

# Holden Caulfield and American Protest

JOYCE ROWE

ON a gray winter afternoon Holden Caulfield, frozen to the quick by more than icy weather, crosses a country road and feels he is disappearing. This image of a bleak moral climate which destroys the soul is not only the keynote of J. D. Salinger's *The Catcher in the Rye* but of much that now seems representative of the general tone of American cultural commentary in the aftermath of World War Two, when the novel was conceived. By 1951 (the year of *Catcher's* publication) the ambiguities of the cold war, of American global power and influence, were stimulating a large popular audience to find new relevance in well-worn images of disaffection from the modern world. These, which historically had been identified with an aesthetic or intellectual elite, were increasingly being adapted to popular taste as they bore on current social and political concerns. The impact of David Riesman's classic sociological study, *The Lonely Crowd,* published one year before *Catcher,* may have paved the way for a new public concern with the disturbing subject of American character; but the immediate interest Riesman's book aroused and its relatively large sale suggest a readership already sensitized to the kind of anomie which Riesman described and from which Holden Caulfield suffers.[1]

In a sense, Salinger's novel functions at a crossroads, a point on an aesthetic and spiritual journey that he was soon to leave behind.[2] Not unlike the author of *David Copperfield* and *Oliver Twist,* whom he is all too anxious to mock, Salinger created a work that is rich enough in language, reference, and scene to captivate innocent and sophisticated readers alike. Indeed, it is only through the democratic nature of his audience that Salinger achieves any version of that ideal community of sensibility and response whose essential absence determines Holden's resistance to the world as it is.[3]

Putting aside the many pleasures of authorial wit, narrative skill, and aesthetic energy that are the first fruits of a reading of *Catcher,* I want to concentrate on a perspective which, thus far, has not received any real critical scrutiny. This is Salinger's ability to infuse a rather formulaic disaffection not merely with the tormented urgency of an individual adolescent voice, but with a resonance that suggests much about the contemporary state of traditional American ideals and aspirations. Holden's brand of alienation gains in significance when viewed not only laterally, in relation to contemporary styles of resistance (as many critics have already done), but historically, in its relation to and displacement of cultural themes which had preoccupied many earlier American writers.[4] To trace such a pattern is, I hope, to deepen our sensitivity to the role that literature plays in shaping the social and moral options that define identity in an historical culture.

Like earlier social resisters in American literature, Holden holds to his own vision of authenticity in the teeth of a morally degraded society. Unlike his forebears, however, he has little faith in either nature or the power of his dreams to compensate for what his "own environment [cannot] supply."[5] The "perfect exhilaration" that Emerson once felt, crossing the snow puddles of Concord Common at twilight, has been transmuted in Holden's urban, modern consciousness to a puzzled speculation: periodically he "wonders" where the ducks in Central Park go in winter when the lagoon in which they live freezes over.[6] The contrast of freezing and freedom, a keynote of Salinger's style, reminds us that the spiritual freedom traditionally symbolized by migratory birds is the remotest of possibilities for Holden. From beginning to end of his journey, from school to sanitarium, Holden's voice, alternating between obscenity and delicacy, conveys his rage at the inability of his contemporaries to transcend the corrosive materialism of modern American life. Many critics have berated him for being a rebel without a cause, asking, in Maxwell Geismar's words, "But what does he argue *for?*"[7] But this inability to move forward and assert a positive goal would seem to be precisely the point of his character.

Difference in Salinger

Rage w/ society

As a precocious but socially impotent upper-middle-class adolescent who is entirely dependent upon institutions that have failed him, Holden has none of the resources – spiritual, economic, or vocational – that might enable him to become Thoreau's "majority of one." In Thoreau's claim that each of us can become a sovereign unit if we act according to the dictates of conscience, we have a classic American "Antinomian" statement, in which the highest form of individualism, of true self-reliance, is to become, paradoxically, an image of the community's best self. *Walden* opens with "Economy," an account of Thoreau's expenditures for building his house, and ends with a vision of spiritual regeneration spreading through the land. In this conception, to rebuild the self is to regenerate the community. Thoreau's Antinomianism is thus not merely a private or eccentric choice but one that manages to fuse all elements of experience – aesthetic, spiritual, social, national – into a unified endeavor. All need not go to the woods, but all must live as if they had discovered Walden Pond within themselves. Although Holden, lacking faith in the power of self-regeneration, is no Thoreau, neither is his dilatory rebellion merely the measure of his own eccentricity. It too symbolizes a pervasive social failure. Like Pencey Prep, an elite boarding school full of crooks, materialist America desecrates and debases whatever falls to its care. A society that had once expressed its redemptive hopes in symbols of great moral or millennial power – Winthrop's City on the Hill, Melville's *Pequod* going down with a "living part of heaven" nailed to its mast – now finds its goals in the platitudes of "adjustment" psychology and the regenerative therapeutic of the sanitarium. What, indeed, is it *for?*

In Holden's postwar lexicon, America and the world are interchangeable terms. And American global hegemony is given its due in the "Fuck you" expletives which Holden sees as an ineluctable blight spreading through space and time – from the walls of his sister's school, to the tomb of the Egyptian mummies at the Metropolitan Museum, to his own future gravestone. ("If you had a million years . . . you couldn't rub out even *half* the "Fuck you" signs in the world" [202].) Like Scott Fitzgerald, Salinger envisions American society as a kind of gigantic Midas, frozen at the heart and thus unable to mature. For all its wealth, its members cannot generate enough respect for their own humanity to care either for their past or their future.

But while Holden lacks the moral energy to make resistance signify as an individual action, he shares with his classic forebears (Hester Prynne, Ishmael, Jay Gatsby) an unwillingness to recognize the ambiguous truths of his own nature and his own needs.[8] This lack of self-awareness characteristic of American heroes, this refusal to probe the tangled underbrush where psychological and social claims intertwine, leads to a familiar pattern: a sense of self-versus-world, an awareness so preoccupied with a lost ideal that any real social engagement is evaded. Thus, paradoxically, rebellion only reinforces the status quo.

Holden's evasion is embodied in a strategy familiar to those who recognize that when Huck Finn lights out for "the Territory" he is making a bid for a hopeless hope – freedom from human contingency; and that when Nick Carraway returns to the West he is following the same path to an unrepeatable past that he has consciously rejected in the pattern of Gatsby's life. Like these dreamers, Holden too is committed to a hopeless vision that makes all the more acute his disgust with the actual. But, in comparison to his forebears, Holden's ideal is a far more diminished thing. It lies in a sunlit childhood Eden, dominated by the image of his dead brother, Allie, who stands for whatever is most authentic in Holden's inner life. Unlike Gatsby, who sacrifices himself to his passion for the past, Holden cannot deceive himself: there is no resurrecting the past, because Allie is dead. This hard fact reduces what was in Gatsby a buoyant, if misguided, hope, to a barren and ineffectual nostalgia. As a mordant comment on American dreamers, it is the last twist of the knife.

Allie's death occurred when Holden was thirteen, the age when puberty begins. On Allie's side of the border it is still childhood, a time when self and world seem, at least in memory, to exist in an enchanted unity. The painful rupture of this sense of self-completion by adolescent self-consciousness and self-doubt is figured in Holden's ritual smashing of the garage window panes at the news of Allie's death. The fact that Holden breaks his own hand in the act – a kind of punitive self-sacrifice – only underscores its symbolic relation to the greater self-mutilation which the loss of childhood signifies for him. The psychic wilderness into which he falls leaves him in a state of continuous nervous anxiety – of being and belonging nowhere, of acute vulnerability to the aggressions and depredations of others against his now-diminished sense of self. But this anxiety never catalyzes any recognition of the enormity of his needs, or of the inevitable limitations of his character. By the end of the story Holden does realize that his vision of himself as catcher was only a daydream. He cannot save either himself or those he loves. ("The thing with kids is, . . . If they fall off, they fall off, but it's bad if you say anything to them" [211].) But this hard-won insight – sustained through his feeling for his little sister Phoebe – is as close as Holden ever comes to establishing any reciprocity with others, or any awareness of the imperatives that operate in their lives.

The notion of the fall into experience as spiritual castration or social betrayal – the dark legacy of romanticism – has had particular importance for those American artists who have viewed American experience from the vantage point of the country's historic ideals. Of course, among those writers we term "classic" there are distinctions to be made. In "The May-Pole of Merry Mount" Hawthorne allegorized adulthood in terms of the marriage ritual, whereby a man and a woman, brought to moral consciousness through their feeling for one another, sublimate the primitive passions of childhood in the social responsibilities of communal life.[9] But Hawthorne's view of the potential for human happiness in adult life (which becomes his own form of idealism) is something of an exception to the more common, albeit complex, ambivalence of nineteenth-century American writers toward the value of what Wordsworth called "the still sad music of humanity" – a melody which can be heard only by those who relinquished their longing for the intuitive glories of childhood.

Indeed, as the century wears on and industrial society assumes its characteristic modern shape, the American sense of despair at and revulsion from the norms of adult life seems to increase. Writers as diverse in sensibility, experience, and social orientation as Dreiser, Wharton, and Hemingway have created, in *Sister Carrie, The House of Mirth,* and *The Sun Also Rises,* works that are remarkably congruent in their protagonists' ultimate response to their world.

Hurstwood, disintegrating under the pressure of his confused longings, can find solace only in the rhythmic motion of his rocking chair pulled close to the warmth of the radiator. Similarly, Lily Bart, overcome by her tortuous social battles, seeks a lost primal warmth by imagining herself cradling a baby in her arms as she relapses into a final narcoticized sleep; and Jake Barnes, made impotent by the war, is unable to imagine a way out of that no-man's-land of lost souls whose wayward pleasures postpone forever the psychosexual dilemmas of adult life. In one form or another, the regression to childhood serves as an "over-determined" response to the limitations of social and individual reality confronting these protagonists. So Holden, praying to the image of his dead brother, fights to hold onto what he fears most to have lost, struggling through a barren present peopled by Stradlaters and Ackleys – "slobs" secret or pathetically overt; moral ciphers who exploit by arrogance or by whining manipulation. The bathos of American society turns out to be the real illness from which Holden suffers. In the degree to which we respond to his voice, to the bid his apostrophes make for our allegiance, his condition of loneliness and longing becomes a mirror of our own predicament.

What Holden shares with, indeed inherits from, such classic American prototypes as the new man of Emerson's essays, the narrator of *Walden,* or of "Song of Myself," or of *Adventures of Huckleberry Finn,* is both a way of perceiving reality – a "horizon of expectations," in the words of E. H. Gombrich – and a way of speaking that enforces this view on the reader/auditor by discrediting or delimiting all potentially competing voices.[10] Both his overt aggression and his more subtle hostility toward others are regularly redeemed by the vitality of his compassion, intelligence, and wit. The reader, like one of Holden's loyal though exasperated teachers, is continually persuaded to acknowledge Holden's innate superiority to those around him. All his conflicts seem designed to reinforce this persuasion, to bind the reader closer to him. The startling intimacy of his address, beginning with "If you really want to hear about it," but quickly becoming "You should have been there," "You would have liked it," flatters the reader by implying that he or she shares in Holden's delicacies of feeling and taste. In effect, the reader fills the space that Allie's death leaves vacant, his silent allegiance the token of an ideal communion in which Holden might find his authenticity confirmed. Indeed, Holden's idiosyncratic friendship with the reader compensates proleptically for the final loss he suffers in freeing his sister from her sacrificial loyalty to him. But such an "ideal communion," demanding nothing less than the absolute acceptance and mutual joy of his lost relations with Phoebe and Allie, leads to a profound distortion of the reciprocal norm implied in the term. By trying to convert us to his way of seeing and feeling – incorporating us, as it were, into his consciousness while distancing himself from others – Holden unconsciously makes clear that such a bond could never be the basis for the dialogic tensions, sympathies, and re-visions upon which real community depends.

Although Holden's consciousness, like that of all first-person narrators, is the lens through which we view his world, it does not follow that the perspective which the reader shares with the narrator must be as restricted as it is here. Not that Holden is so thoroughly reliable that we cannot see his own confusions and pretensions; there are obvious discrepancies between what he says about himself and the truth of his situation and feelings. His boarding school precocity masks a vulnerability to social humiliation; his pride in his looks and intelligence does little to assuage his guilty fascination with and fear of female sexuality; and his displaced aggression only underscores his doubts about his own sexual potency. But these effects are all too obvious. They exist not for the sake of challenging or complicating our empathy with Holden, but of reinforcing it by humanizing him with the same falsities and fears, the same ambiguous mix of "crumby" and decent impulses, that we can accept in ourselves. They make us like him better, believe in his innate decency as we wish to believe in our own, and so encourage us to accept his view of experience as an adequate response to the world. Indeed Holden, "confused, frightened and . . . sickened" by the behavior of others, flatters the reader's sense of his own moral acumen; it is all too easy to accept Holden as an exemplar of decency in an indecent age.

Although Holden claims that in telling his tale he has come to "miss" Ackley, Maurice, and the others, his presentation of these figures hardly suggests a deep engagement with the substance of their lives. Like Thoreau's Walden neighbors, whose prodigal habits are introduced only to reinforce the superiority of the narrator's "economy," the characters that Holden meets have little depth apart from their function as specimens of a depressingly antithetical world. If one cares about the three female tourists from Seattle with whom Holden tries to dance, it must be for the sake of one's own humanity, not theirs. They are like flies on the wall of Holden's consciousness – their own histories or motivations need not trouble us. Thus Holden's plunge into the urban muddle, while it seems to provide images of the social complexity of modern America, turns out to be a curiously homogeneous affair: each class or type merely serves as another reflection of a predetermined mental scheme. In this hall of mirrors the apparent multiplicity of experience turns out to be largely a replication of the same experience, in which those who act out of purpose, conviction, or faith are heartbreakingly rare.

empathy

In place of authenticity Holden finds an endless appetite for the glamour of appearance, for the vanity of effect and approval. The story that he writes for Stradlater about the poems on Allie's baseball mitt is rejected by his "unscrupulous" roommate because it doesn't follow the rules of the English composition assignment: "'You don't do *one damn thing* the way you're supposed to,'" says the infuriated Stradlater. "'Not one damn thing'"(1). Holden, of course, resists the rules in order to explore his own nascent artistic integrity, while around him those with more claim to our respect than the obtuse Stradlater betray talent and spirit alike by modeling themselves on one another and conforming their behavior to the regulations of a standardized "performance."

Ernie, the talented "colored" piano player who runs his own New York nightclub, is a case in point. He has learned to capture the attention of his customers by performing before a spotlighted mirror. His face, not his *fingers,* as Holden points out, is the focus of his style. Once very good, he now parodies himself and packs in the customers who, themselves anxiously performing for one another, applaud Ernie wildly. "I don't even think he *knows* any more when he's playing right or not," Holden says (84). Holden's sense of artistry thus serves as a measure of all false values. To the degree that we endorse his authenticity we, who would "puke" along with him, are enabled to share it.

Because there is no other character in the book to provide serious commentary on, or resistance to, Holden's point of view, his experience lacks the kind of dialectical opposition, or reciprocal sympathy, through which he, and we, might develop a more complex sense of the imperatives of American social reality. As he says about the abortive attempt of Mr. Spencer to focus his attention on his failed history exam: "I felt sorry as hell for him. . . . But I just couldn't hang around there any longer, the way we were on opposite sides of the pole . . ." (15). It is this need to polarize and abstract all personal relations that defeats any possibility of normative social connection and engagement. Though Holden complains that people "never give your message to anybody," that "people never notice anything," it is his dominating consciousness, setting himself and the reader in a world apart, that insures his isolation.

Holden's continuous need to defend himself from the encroachments of others generates the verbal disguise he uses to fictionalize all his encounters with adults. The games he plays with Mr. Spencer and Mrs. Morrow, "shooting the bull," telling each what he thinks will most interest and please, enable him to distance himself from the false self his false phrases create as he attempts to protect the true core of his being. As the psychoanalyst D. W. Winnicott has described it, "the true self" is a core of identity which is always invulnerable to external reality and never communicates with it. In adolescence, "That which is truly personal and which feels real must be defended at all cost." Winnicott's description of what violation of its integrity means to the true self – "Rape and being eaten by cannibals . . . are mere bagatelles" by comparison – brings to mind the emotional horror that Hawthorne displays toward the violation of another's deepest self, which he calls the Unpardonable Sin.[11] This sense of an integrity to be defended at all cost shapes the Antinomianism, as it does the duality, of Hester Prynne, Huck Finn, and Melville's most notable protagonists. But unlike these forebears, whose need for self-protection is clearly denoted by their double lives, Holden has very little inner or secret freedom in which to function. If society is a prison, then, as in a nightmare tale of Poe, the walls have moved inward, grazing the captive's skin.

Seen in this light, Holden's constant resort to obscenity serves as a shield, a perverse rite of purification that protects him from the meretricious speech of others, which threatens his very existence. Language, for Holden, is a moral matter. In the tradition of Puritan plain-speech, which has had such a marked influence on American prose style, the authenticity of the word derives from, as it points toward, the authenticity of the mind and heart of the speaker. But unlike the narrators of *Walden* and "Song of Myself," who give voice to a language fully commensurate with their visionary longings, Holden's imprecations and expletives ultimately serve to define his impotence; they reveal the degree to which he is already contaminated by the manners, institutions, and authorities of his society. The inadequacy of his vocabulary, upon which he himself remarks ("I have a lousy vocabulary" [9]) is a reflection not merely of his adolescent immaturity, but of the more abiding impoverishment from which he as a representative hero suffers – the inability to conceptualize any form of social reciprocity, of a reasonably humane community, in which the "true self" might feel respected and therefore safe. Lacking such faith there is finally nothing that Holden can win the reader to but complicity in disaffection.[12]

It is a literary commonplace that the English novel – from Austen, Dickens, and Conrad to writers of our own day, like Iris Murdoch – has regularly focused its critical energies on the interrelation of social institutions and individual character. In the work of English and European writers generally, society is the ground of human experience. Although many English protagonists enter their stories as orphans, their narratives lead toward a kind of self-recognition or social accommodation to others that represents the evolving meaning of their experience. One grows, develops, changes through interactions with others in a web of social and personal forces which is simply life itself.

But classic American heroes never make such accommodations. Their identities are shaped, not by interaction with others but in resistance to whatever *is*, in the name of a higher social, ethical, or aesthetic ideal. This, as I have noted, is the ground of their Antinomianism – a public or exemplary heroism, designed to be the only morally respectable position in the narrative. Orphanhood has functioned quite differently for American heroes than for European. More than a starting point from which the hero must evolve a social and moral identity, it represents a liberation from the past that is a totalizing condition of existence – spiritual, psychological, political, and metaphysical. American heroes, seemingly alone, free, and without family or history, test the proposition that a new world might bring a new self and society into being. Although in each case the hero's or heroine's effort issues in failure, there is no conventional recognition of this experiential truth on the part of the protagonist, no willingness to recalculate his or her relations to society or history. American individualism thus reshapes the archetypal pattern of the orphaned young man (or woman) seeking an adult identity by coming to terms with him or herself in the matrix of family life.

Indeed, the family, as the basis for individual as well as social identity, hardly exists in classic nineteenth-century American literature. Almost invariably American heroes lack the memory of past roots. Hawthorne's *The Scarlet Letter* is perhaps the proof text for this statement. Hester Prynne, having shed her European past, stands before the Puritan community, her infant in her arms, unwilling to identify the father – a revelation that would establish a new family (in Hester's ideal terms) on these shores. The fact that Pearl returns to Europe at the story's end, that Dimmesdale tortures himself to death rather than acknowledge his paternity, and that Hester herself remains alone, dreaming of the New World community yet to be, suggests how thoroughly discouraged this most "social" of our classic novelists was about the prospects for authentic family relations in American society.

American heroes like Ishmael and Gatsby are fatherless by choice as well as circumstance. Ishmael will continue to wander as he searches for his lost homeland; Gatsby reaches toward an impossible transcendence whose measure lies precisely in its ineffable difference from the world he knows. Thus Holden's initial dismissal of family history as "all that David Copperfield kind of crap" suggests his affinity with the traditional American rejection of the kind of bildungsroman which *David Copperfield,* among other Dickens novels, exemplifies. But while Holden fully shares, on the deepest spiritual level, in the isolation of the traditional American hero, nothing enforces our sense of his impotence more than his ineffectual play at orphanhood in an urban wilderness. Enmeshed as he is in a labyrinth of social roles and family expectations, escape – to a sunny cabin near, but not in the woods – is envisaged in terms of a cliché whose eerie precision illuminates the core of desperation that sustains the image. Salinger's hero is wedded to a pattern of thought and aspiration in which he can no longer seriously believe. He invokes it because it is the only form of self-affirmation his culture affords.

If the old dream of regeneration through separation has become both terrifying and foolish, society remains for Holden what it has always been for American heroes – an anti-community which continues to betray its own high birthright for a mess of commercial pottage. Holden's fear of disappearing – an image which joins the beginning and end of the story – as he crosses from one side of the road or street to the other, aptly expresses his sense of the diminishing ground for authenticity in America. The peculiar sense of a materialism so blanketing that it produces a pervasive deadening of affect becomes the mark of the age. One thinks of Sylvia Plath's *The Bell Jar,* whose heroine finds a correlative to the terror of inner emptiness in the social sterility of Madison Avenue glamour – just that world which Holden imagines himself as headed for. Books such as *The Man in the Grey Flannel Suit* and *Sincerely, Willis Wayde,* written to attract a large popular audience, turn these perceptions into the simplified, world-weary clichés of growing up and selling out.[13] But whether cynical or sincere, the protagonists of these novels share with Holden an inability to conceptualize the future as anything but a dead end. "It didn't seem like *any*thing was coming" (118), says Holden, conveying the sense of a world that seems to annihilate the possibility of growth.

Trying to imagine himself a lawyer like his father, Holden wonders if his father knows why he does what he does. Holden knows that lawyers who rake in the cash don't go around saving the innocent. But even if you were such an idealistic fellow, "how would you know if you did it because you really *wanted* to save guys' lives, or because what you really *wanted* to do was be a terrific lawyer, with everybody slapping you on the back and congratulating you in court . . . " (172). In a society as replete with verbal falsities as this one, how do you trust your own words, your own thoughts? How do you know when you are telling yourself the truth?

Dickens's tales also show adolescence in an urban commercial society to be a dislocating and frightening process. But from *Nicholas Nickleby* through *Great Expectations* there is regularly a kindly, decent figure who provides aid, comfort, and tutelage in time of need. However bad the adult world seems, enough sources of social strength remain to make the protagonist's struggle toward maturity worthwhile. But Holden never finds such an adult. Mr. Spencer, the history teacher who *seems* to take a fatherly interest in him, is actually most interested in shaming and humiliating him. D.B., the older brother he admires, is as emotionally remote from him as is his father, and Holden takes revenge by reviling him for "selling out" to Hollywood. His mother, as he repeatedly notes, is too nervous and anxious herself to do more than pay perfunctory attention to her children's needs. His father is a shadowy abstraction – a corporate lawyer, defined by his preoccupations and vexations. We hear from Phoebe that "Daddy's going to kill you," rather than experience the father directly through any memory of Holden's.

Holden's anxiety, then, is of a specifically contemporary kind. Those adults who should serve as moral tutors and nurturers are neither wholly absent nor fully present. Perhaps, as David Riesman puts it in speaking of middle-class American parents, "they are passing on to him their own contagious, highly diffuse anxiety," as they look to others to define values and goals increasingly based upon socially approved ephemera.[14] Yet, however shadowy these adult figures may be, they are as controlling of Holden as is the impersonal, elusive corporate authority which, he knows, ultimately determines the values of his home. Like the corporate structure itself, these adults are profoundly ambiguous figures whose seeming beneficence it is dangerous to trust. All are effectively epitomized in the teacher Mr. Antolini, whose paternal decency may be entwined with a predator's taste for young boys, and whose advice to Holden turns out to be as puzzling, if not as specious, as his midnight hospitality.

Remarking that Holden is a natural student, Mr. Antolini urges education on him for its efficiency: "After a while, you'll have an idea what kind of thoughts your particular size mind should be wearing. For one thing, it may save you an extraordinary amount of time trying on ideas that . . . aren't becoming to you. You'll begin to know your true measurements and dress your mind accordingly." Mr. Antolini's words, like his manners, are glibly seductive, and a trifle coarse. Ideas as garments that one slips on for the fit – a ready-made identity – is a concept not far removed from the kind of stylized performance that Holden detects in the Lunts ("they were *too* good") and Ernie. It is suited to a society that increasingly emphasizes image and appearance as intrinsically valuable; a society in which the mess and pain of a real struggle with ideas and feelings is considered an unwelcome deviation from the approved norm of "personality."

Because Holden's final return to his family, his "going home," is never dramatized, we are deprived of the experience of a reckoning in which some genuine moral insight, in distinction to Mr. Antolini's sartorial version in the quest for knowledge, might occur. Instead, we are left with the sense of a society that Holden can neither accept nor escape. His encounter has only served to increase his sense of himself as a creature at bay. His anxiety is never allayed.

Because Holden is never allowed to imagine or experience himself in any significant struggle with others (his bloody fistfight with Stradlater emphasizes the futility of any gesture that *is* open to him), neither he (nor his creator) can conceive of society as a source of growth, or self-knowledge. In place of a dialectical engagement with others, Holden clings to the kind of inner resistance that keeps exiles and isolates alive. In response to the pressures for "adjustment" which his sanitarium psychiatrists impose, he insists upon the principle that spontaneity and life depend upon "not knowing what you're going to *do* until you do it" (213). If the cost of this shard of freedom is the continuing anxiety which alienation and disaffection bring – of life in a permanent wilderness, so to speak – so be it. Impoverished it may be, but in Holden's sense of "freedom" one can already see foreshadowed the celebrated road imagery of the Beats.

Holden's struggle for a moral purity that the actual corruptions and compromises of American society, or indeed any society, belie is a familiar one to readers of classic American works. But as I have already suggested, for Holden the terms of that struggle are reversed. Unlike nineteenth-century characters, Holden is not an obvious social outsider or outcast to those he lives among. Well-born and well-favored, his appearance, abilities, and manners make him an insider – he belongs. And yet, as the heir of all the ages, blessed with the material splendors of the Promised Land, Holden feels more victim or prisoner than favored son. Like the country at large, he expresses his discomfort, his sense of dis-ease, by squandering his resources – physical, emotional, intellectual – without attempting to utilize them for action and change. But the willful futility of his acts should not blind us to the psychic truth which they reveal. Ultimately Holden is performing a kind of self-mutilation against that part of himself which is hostage to the society that has shaped him. Moreover, while previous American heroes like Hester Prynne and Huck Finn evaded social reality at the cost of denying their human need for others and their likeness to them, Holden's resistance concludes on a wistful note of longing for everybody outside the prison of his sanitarium – an ambivalence that aptly fixes the contemporary terms of his predicament.

Holden's self-division is thus reduced to the only form in which his society can bear to consider it – a psychological problem of acceptance and adjustment; yet Salinger's irony results in a curious double focus. The increasing prestige of American psychoanalysis in the 1950s may be attributed to its tendency (at least in the hands of some practitioners) to sever individual issues and conflicts from their connections to more obdurate realities in the social world. There is familiar comfort in the belief that *all* problems are ultimately individual ones which can, at least potentially, be resolved by force of the individual mind and will. This irony surely lies within the compass of Salinger's story.[15] But its effect is undercut by the polarized perspective that Salinger has imposed on his hero. As we have seen, the stoic isolation through which Holden continues to protect his authenticity is itself an ethic that devalues confrontation or action and so fixes human possibility in the mold of a hopeless hope. Indeed, it becomes a strategy for containment, as much an evasion of social reality as is the psychiatric imperative to adjust.

There is nothing finally in Holden's diffuse sympathies to offend or dismay the reader, nothing to keep him permanently on edge. By the end of the story the reader has seen his familiar social world questioned, shaken, only to be reconstituted as an inevitable fate.[16] Having been drawn to Holden's side we are finally drawn to his mode of perception and defense. To keep the citadel of the self intact by keeping others at a distance is the kind of social agreement that guarantees that the longed-for community which American experience forever promises will surely forever be withheld.

In discussing the romantic novelist in nineteenth-century European literature, René Girard remarks that the romantic establishes a Manichean division of self and other, refusing to see how "Self is implicated in Other." But since Gerard's concern is as much with the author as with the characters, he goes on to note that this situation is finally attributable to the novelist who stands behind the character and refuses to free either himself or his character from these limitations. In distinction, a "classic" novelist, such as Cervantes, transcends this opposition by distancing himself from his character and so frees himself from the character's perspective. Some form of reconciliation is then possible between protagonist and world.[17]

In Girard's terms, Salinger never frees himself, or therefore the reader, from the grip of Holden's perspective. What happens is just the reverse. We are initiated into a process of seeing in which we are either on the side of integrity and autonomy (Holden) or on the side of the predators and exploiters – from Maurice the pimp to the anonymous psychoanalyst who wants Holden to promise to "apply" himself. A Manichean choice indeed. For the reader, this duality preempts all other modes of perception. The corrosive materialism that blasts Holden as it does his world finally becomes irrelevant to any particular historical moment or reality. Instead, isolation, anxiety, the modern sickness of soul turns out to be the given, irremediable condition of our lives.

## NOTES

1. David Riesman, with Reuel Denny and Nathan Glazer, *The Lonely Crowd: A Study of the Changing American Character* (New Haven: Yale University Press, 1950). By 1967 the book was in its thirteenth printing. An abridged version (New York: Doubleday, Anchor Press, 1955) has been widely available ever since, though I have not been able to obtain exact sales figures. Riesman derives the term anomie from the French sociologist Emile Durkheim's *anomique,* "meaning ruleless, ungoverned." But Riesman uses it in a broader sense than did Durkheim. For Riesman, anomic individuals are out in the cold, caught between the more desirable state of "autonomy" and the blind conformity of the "adjusted" (abridged ed., p. 278). For another perspective on the mass cultural anxieties which can be figured in Riesman's term, see Michael Wood's comments on the imagery of film noir in *America at the Movies* (New York: Basic Books, 1975).
2. For a consideration of the sacramental vision of experience, tentatively broached here, but confidently asserted in the later stories, especially "Raise High the Roof Beam, Carpenters" and "Zooey," see Ihab Hassan, "Almost the Voice of Silence: The Later Novellettes of J. D. Salinger," *Wisconsin Studies in Contemporary Literature* 4, no. 1 (Winter 1963).
3. In 1965 *Catcher* was listed as one of ten leading mass-market paperback bestsellers. In 1967 it was one of "the leading twenty-five best sellers since 1895" (*Facts on File,* quoted in Jack R. Sublette, *J. D. Salinger: An Annotated Bibliography, 1938–1981* [New York: Garland Publishing Co., 1984], p. 132). It has not been possible to obtain current sales figures, but the book still seems to be a perennial favorite among high school students. In a personal survey, every one of the college freshmen in my required English course (two sections, seventy students) was familiar with it.
4. Two well-known views that place Holden in his own time suggest the range of many others. Maxwell Geismar ("J. D. Salinger: The Wise Child and *The New Yorker* School of Fiction," in *American Moderns: From Rebellion to Conformity* [New York: Hill and Wang, 1958]) exclaims that "The *Catcher in the Rye* protests, to be sure, against both the academic and social conformity of its period. But what does it argue *for?*" Contemptuous of what he detects as a faked Anglicized patina, glossing a deracinated Jewish world, Geismar dismisses the novel's perspective as "well-to-do and neurotic anarchism" (p. 198). David Galloway (*The Absurd Hero in American Fiction* [Austin: University of

Texas Press, 1966]), far more sympathetic to Holden's plight, finds it readily assimilable to his own existentialist concerns. "Holden doesn't refuse to grow up so much as he agonizes over the state of being grown up." He stands for modern man (frustrated, disillusioned, anxious) – a "biting image of the absurd contemporary milieu" (p. 145). While Holden may indeed stand for modern man, I find Galloway's argument, from absurdity to frustration, to be a circular one. The question remains: why should this time be more absurd than any other time; why must frustration be predicated upon absurdity? Holden has often been compared (unfavorably) to Huck Finn. But these comparisons are essentially limited to differences in character and social scene. The deeper structural and thematic affinities between *Catcher* and earlier "classic" American works have either been ignored or dissipated in the generalities characteristic of the transcultural myth criticism so popular in the 1950s and 1960s. For an example of the latter, see Arthur Heiserman and James E. Miller, Jr., "J. D. Salinger: Some Crazy Cliff," *Western Humanities Review* 10 (Spring 1956): 129–37.

5. *The Catcher in the Rye* (New York: Bantam, 1964.), p. 187. All quotations will be from this edition and hereinafter will be cited in parentheses.
6. Ralph Waldo Emerson, *The Collected Works*, Alfred R. Ferguson, general editor (Cambridge, Mass.: Belknap Press of Harvard University, 1971), vol. 1, p. 10.
7. Geismar, *American Moderns*, p. 198. See also Mary McCarthy, "J. D. Salinger's Closed Circuit," *Harper's Magazine* 225 (October 1962): 46–7.
8. See the introduction to my *Equivocal Endings in Classic American Novels* (Cambridge University Press, 1988) for an outline of the pattern this resistance takes in classic American novels.
9. Nathaniel Hawthorne, *Centenary Edition of Collected Works*, ed. William Charvat and others (Columbus: Ohio State University Press, 1963–1985), vol. 9, pp. 54–67.
10. E. H. Gombrich, *Art and Illusion: A Study in the Psychology of Pictorial Representation* (Princeton: Princeton University Press, 1960), p. 60.
11. D. W. Winnicott, *The Maturational Process and the Facilitating Environment* (New York: The International Universities Press, 1965), pp. 190, 187. Winnicott stresses the value of isolation to the adolescent: "Preservation of personal isolation is part of the search for identity and for the establishment of a personal technique for communicating which does not lead to violation of the central self" (p. 190). The difficulty for Holden is that his culture offers no support for his struggle; it is as

if the subject of identity has become such a chronic and pervasive cultural dilemma, generating so much anxiety, that the adolescent adults who surround him treat the problem (as his mother does) like a headache they have learned to live with and ignore.

12. Unusual among early critical responses to *Catcher* is Hansford Martin's "The American Problem of Direct Address," *Western Review* 16 (Winter 1952): 101–14. Martin notes that American writers almost invariably are concerned with the problem of voice, of "man-talking-to-you." He calls this "a literature of direct address," but attributes the phenomenon wholly to the artist's democratic concern with the interaction between art and society (p. 101).
13. Sloan Wilson, *The Man in the Grey Flannel Suit* (New York: Simon and Schuster, 1955); John P. Marquand, *Sincerely, Willis Wayde* (Boston: Little, Brown, 1955);Sylvia Plath, *The Bell Jar* (1963; rpt. New York: Bantam, 1971).
14. Riesman, *The Lonely Crowd*, p. 49.
15. Compare John Cheever's 1958 story, "The Country Husband," in *The Housebreaker of Shady Hill and Other Stories* (New York: Harper and Brothers, 1958), pp. 49–84. Similarly, the husband ends in the basement, devoted to his psychiatrically prescribed woodworking therapy as a cure for his unnameable angst.
16. Cf. Carol and Richard Ohmann, "Reviewers, Critics, and *The Catcher in the Rye*," *Critical Inquiry* 3, no. 1 (Autumn 1976): 15–38. The Ohmanns review previous critics to point out how Salinger's precise social criticism has been generalized to deny its topical force. They object to the general critical response that Holden's predicament has been left to him to solve, as a problem of more love, the search for identity, and so forth. Instead, the Ohmanns stress specific bourgeois capitalist relations, hypocrisies of class and exploitation to which they find Holden responding. While the Ohmanns rightly, I believe, assert that "the novel draws readers into a powerful longing for what-could-be, and at the same time interposes what-is as an unchanging and immovable reality," they readily attribute to Salinger a political aim ("these values cannot be realized within extant social forms" [p. 35]) that is really their own. The critics who have read Holden's problem as his alone may indeed have missed a good deal of Salinger's social criticism, but, as I have tried to show, Salinger creates the ambiguity. In the end, the book offers ample warrant for just this kind of individualistic interpretation.
17. René Girard, *Deceit, Desire, and the Novel* (Baltimore: Johns Hopkins University Press, 1966), pp. 271, 308.

6

# Love and Death in *The Catcher in the Rye*

PETER SHAW

BY the time *The Catcher in the Rye* appeared in 1951, the theme of the sensitive youth beleaguered by society was well established in the American novel. Reviewing Truman Capote's *Other Voices, Other Rooms* in 1948, Diana Trilling complained about the tendency of contemporary novelists to employ a "deterministic principle" in which the youth was repeatedly presented as a "passive victim." Also well established by 1951 was the link between neurosis, self-destructive behavior, and social maladaptation on the one hand, and artistic sensibility and special insight on the other. Not surprisingly, Holden Caulfield was regarded as yet another fictional example of the sensitive, outcast character vouchsafed a superior insight by a touch of mental disturbance.

Holden's disturbance was taken to be both his unique, personal gift and the fault of a hypocritical, uncaring society, one particularly indifferent to its more sensitive souls. Holden's insight into the adult world's hypocrisies, moreover, appeared to derive precisely from his being its casualty. Given the deplorable world in which he lived, if by the end of his adventures Holden seemed ready to effect some kind of accommodation with society, this struck readers as inevitable, if regrettable.

It is certainly true that like other of Salinger's youths, Holden properly belongs to the contemporary American novel's procession of sensitive, psychologically crippled but superior characters. Nevertheless, he is not simply a product of the deterministic principle observed by Trilling and endorsed by the commentators of the fifties. If Holden is a casualty of society, he is also a psychological case in his own right. Moreover, he is presented in a somewhat different manner than are the sentimentalized young people in other novels of his period. In the first place his critique of society is by no means entirely endorsed, and in the second his eventual accommodation to society is by no means presented as a capitulation.

It has not gone unnoticed that Holden is virtually a case study. He writes his account from a mental institution, has a morbid preoccupation with death, and comes perilously close to a nervous breakdown while walking up Fifth Avenue. In the intellectual climate of the 1950s, these circumstances hardly told against a fictional character. As Mrs. Trilling had put it a few years earlier, "a considerable section of our literary culture" held the view that "madness is a normal, even a better than normal, way of life."[1] In the same spirit, the first full-scale and still probably the most widely accepted academic essay on *The Catcher in the Rye,* written in the mid-1950s, concluded:

> It is not Holden who should be examined for a sickness of the mind, but the world in which he has sojourned and found himself an alien. To "cure" Holden, he must be given the contagious, almost universal disease of phony adultism.[2]

The word *cure* in quotation marks expresses the view that mental health and illness are misleading terms that should, if anything, be reversed. On the other hand, the expression "phony adultism" indicates that rather than being an endorsement of true madness, this typical fifties defense of Holden amounts to little more than a way of stigmatizing American society for its stuffiness and insensitivity to exceptional spirits. Not until the 1960s, with R. D. Laing's elevation of the clinical schizophrenic to prophetic status, would actual madness come to be endorsed as superior to normality.

Not surprisingly, one early review of *The Catcher in the Rye* characterized Holden's alienation and obsessions as examples of the routine and familiar difficulties of adolescence: they added up to "a case history of all of us."[3] The implication was that as adolescents "all of us," disturbed by the insensitivities and vulgarities of contemporary life, have felt that we were going crazy. Other critics soon went so far as to endorse Holden in whatever degree of mental disturbance he might be said to suffer. Yet in the cultural atmosphere of the 1950s, the feeling that Holden was ultimately normal coexisted comfortably with the idea of his being psychologically disturbed.

It was not until the 1970s and 1980s, in two essays, that any attempt was made to account for Holden in primarily psychological terms. E. H. Miller wrote in 1982 that "most critics have tended to accept Holden's evaluation of the world as phony, when in fact his attitudes are symptomatic of a serious psychological problem." Miller, "instead of treating the novel as a commentary by an innocent young man rebelling against an insensitive world or as a study of a youth's moral growth," tries to show that Holden's "rebelliousness is his only means of dealing with his inability to come to terms with the death of his brother." In contrast, the other psychoanalytic critic, James Bryan – who theorizes that Holden is ruled by a suppressed incest wish directed toward his ten-year-old sister, Phoebe – does not conclude that Holden's insights are undermined by his having psychological difficulties.[4]

The psychological approach, then, though it insists on a fairly serious diagnosis of Holden, does not definitively establish the grounds either for dismissal or endorsement of his social critique. What it does establish is that Holden's observations and his mental state are manifestly related to one another. The question is, how?

Holden's psychologically disturbed state has been advanced as the source both of his insight and of his lack of insight. The lines have been sharply drawn between Holden as an insightful social critic and as a mistaken projector of his own frailties onto society. Since evidence can be found to support each of these analyses, it might follow that Holden is an inconsistently drawn character. Yet he has never struck readers this way. How, then, can the opposite impressions of consistency and inconsistency in his character be reconciled?

The answer to this question, I wish to argue, lies in the peculiar dynamics of adolescent psychology. The teenage years stand out as life's most complicated and tortured period. It has been said that teenage behavior, with its swings into and out of rationality, actually resembles schizophrenia. Certainly, this is the one period of life in which abnormal behavior is common rather than exceptional. It is no wonder, then, that young readers and professional critics alike have been able to regard Holden as normal despite his own conviction that he is not – or that other readers have been able to regard him primarily as a disturbed youth even though he often talks sense.[5]

Failing to take into account the normality of abnormality in adolescence, the psychoanalytic critics in particular have taken a too purely clinical approach to Holden. E. H. Miller's positing of a life crisis dominated by mourning and guilt over the death of Allie, for example, seems too comprehensive and too definitive. For although Allie's death might be cited to account for much of Holden's behavior, no single act or expression of his stands out as inexplicable without reference to Allie. His brother's death exacerbates rather than constitutes Holden's adolescent crisis.

The psychoanalytic essays rest narrowly on single explanations, and disagree with one another. Nevertheless, their notation of classical symptoms in Holden should make it impossible for critics any longer to ignore the importance of psychological processes in both Holden's behavior and his ideas. Miller, for example, is able to call attention to at least fifty mentions by Holden of being depressed, repeated references on his part to himself and others as "crazy," and "his repeated use of variations on the phrase 'that killed me.' " One can add that Holden's disturbed condition is also evoked by a pattern of verbal slips, double entendres, errors, forgettings, accidents, and fallings down. The most striking of his double entendres, redolent both of guilt over Allie's death and an attempt to fob off that guilt on someone else, is a remark about his sister Phoebe containing the words, "she killed Allie, too." Of course he means by "killed" that she amused Allie. But his unconscious understanding is that Phoebe (like himself) is somehow responsible for Allie's death. Holden reveals that this actual death lies behind his casual use of the word "killed" when he goes on to mention next, apparently irrelevantly, that Phoebe is ten years old. For this is the age at which Allie died.

It can also be added that Holden uses the word "crazy" and its variants *mad, madman,* and *insane* over fifty times – and pretends that he is suffering from a brain tumor. (He actually uses his famous term "phony" less often – approximately forty times.) Such signals of mental distress, it is worth noticing, were even more prominent in a version of the book's opening scene, a story entitled "I'm Crazy," published by Salinger in *Collier's* magazine in 1945. There Holden explains his being out in the cold without coat or gloves: "Only a crazy guy would have stood there. That's me. Crazy. No kidding, I have a screw loose."[6]

As with the rest of his behavior, Holden's self-punishments have some reference to guilt over Allie's death, as well as having a source in adolescent psychology. "The adolescent," writes Peter Blos in *On Adolescence: A Psychoanalytic Interpretation*, "incurs a real loss in the renunciation of his oedipal parents, and he experiences the inner emptiness, grief, and sadness which is part of all mourning." The adolescent also mourns for his own earlier childhood. If *The Catcher in the Rye* is, as E. H. Miller argues, about Holden's need "to bury Allie before he can make the transition to adulthood," it is also about Holden's need to bury and mourn other elements of his past. The elements link up with memories of Allie, pushing Holden toward breakdown yet always rendering his experience recognizable.

But mourning is only one of the two main psychological experiences typical of Holden's stage of adolescence. The other is "being in love." If Holden is unable to move on from mourning, he is equally unable to commence the being-in-love portion of his maturation process. He is suffering through what Erik Erikson calls "the prime danger of this age": an excessively prolonged "moratorium" on growing up. (Such prolongation can also be referred to as a "moratorium of illness.")[7]

Holden expresses his need for moratoriums on both death and love in his two museum visits. The first visit is to the Museum of Natural History, whose dioramas of American Indian life convey an image of time suspended. The Indian who is fishing and the squaw who is weaving will never change, he muses, and he goes on to fantasize returning to the dioramas, without growing older, and finding the figures always exactly the same. Their perfection stands against the disturbing implications of a different couple – Holden's parents. He imagines himself making one of his trips to view the museum figures after hearing his "mother and father having a terrific fight in the bathroom." The mature life of couples, in other words, presents a threatening prospect relieved by contemplating the Indian mother and father in the museum. Their serene sameness evokes an imagined, permanent moratorium on love and its consequences.

At the Metropolitan Museum of Art, Holden leads two little boys to the reconstructed pharaonic tomb and its collection of mummies. When the boys run away in fright at his account of mummification (characteristically the only information about Ancient Egypt he could recall for his history examination), he finds that he "liked it" in the tomb: "it was so nice and peaceful" (183). Here is a place in which he can finally rest in untroubled communion with eternal death: he is alongside mummies preserved as he wishes Allie could be preserved, and symbolizing his own wish to be preserved from change. Very soon, though, like his other moments of suspension, this one is rudely interrupted. He is driven from the tomb when a scrawled "Fuck you" graffito catches his eye. Not for the first time the insistent reminder of sex drives him reluctantly back into life – this time to the bathroom where he faints in a purgative ritual that marks his first emergence from his moratorium.[8]

Holden's clinging to the part of his moratorium that concerns sex is expressed in his curious fondness for his friend Jane Gallagher's keeping her kings in the back row when playing checkers. Jane is the girl he has kissed on only one occasion, but whose date with his roommate makes him frantic, and whom he cannot quite bring himself to phone after he runs away from school. Critics have interpreted Holden's repeated mentions of the kings in the back row as expressions of his own "fear," or as representing "a holding back of one's aggressive powers and an unwillingness to enter the competitive game and use them against other people," or else as an attempt on Holden's part to warn Jane against the sexual intentions of his roommate, Stradlater.[9]

All of these speculations are compatible with the psychology of the moratorium. But at a still deeper level, Jane's withholding her kings may be said to symbolize the suspension of maturation typical of this adolescent period – even as it typifies the static, sexually unthreatening relationship Holden has had with her. For, like young people, the pieces on a checkerboard must keep moving forward. Or, as the game's technical term has it, they must keep "developing." On reaching the back row they have in effect achieved maturity, and are accordingly "kinged." By not moving her kings out of the back row, Jane solves the problem presented by this unavoidable process of maturation. She has made it one of *arrested development.* Understandably, this is particularly attractive to Holden.

Holden's catcher in the rye fantasy is usually understood to contain a kind of moratorium idea. The children falling off the cliff are said to symbolize a fall into adulthood, from which Holden imagines himself sparing them even as he would spare himself. But it is possible to be more specific: in psychological terms the "catcher" passage combines the elements both of falling in love and of mourning. To see how this is so, it is important to notice the source of the fantasy – Holden's watching a couple and their child – in order to track the unconscious allusive trail leading to love and death. Holden recalls walking along Fifth Avenue one day and observing with pleasure and empathy a couple and their playful child. To begin with, the family is not well off, Holden observes. This connects its members to the series of underdogs Holden has been attracted to, starting with fellow students at Pencey Prep, and extending to characters in movies and books. Furthermore, the child, at the moment he is observed, is a kind of outcast in the family itself – "walking alone" while the parents "were just walking along, talking, not paying any attention to their kid."

The child is also in danger. He is walking in the roadway, albeit "right next to the curb." Perilously, "cars zoomed by, brakes screeched all over the place, his parents paid no attention to him, and he kept on walking next to the curb." Clearly, the child's danger prompts the fantasy of rescue in the rye that soon comes into Holden's thoughts. "If a body catch a body coming through the rye," he hears the boy singing, and he begins to imagine himself catching the bodies of children in another kind of danger (105).

Viewing the catcher fantasy psychologically, E. H. Miller puts it that "Holden has the 'crazy' idea that he should have saved Allie." But psychoanalytically speaking, the process leading to the fantasy of rescue would have to be described as somewhat more complicated. The child whose sibling dies commonly suffers not so much the guilt of having failed to effect a rescue as that of having at some time harbored the wish that the sibling might die. (When Allie died, Holden's immediate reaction had been to punish himself by slamming his fist through the garage windows, prompting his parents to think of having him psychoanalyzed.) The actual death, no matter what its cause (Allie had died of leukemia), can lead to a reaction formation, that is, to the creation of an opposite wish. The wish to kill, for example, can be replaced by a wish to rescue. Allie is the source of the rescue fantasy, then, but not its object.

In Holden's case the reaction formation manifested in the catcher fantasy is combined with another kind of guilt that may follow the death of a sibling, that felt by virtue of being a survivor. Such guilt often leads to an avoidance of success – as when Holden repeatedly fails out of schools – or else to imagining oneself incapable of success at an ordinary vocation. Being a catcher in the rye, no ordinary vocation, provides a bridge from guilty failure to success of a psychologically acceptable kind.

The being-in-love aspect of the catcher passage emerges from the prominent but neglected circumstance of its connection with the series of errors and slips revealing of Holden's unconscious. As Phoebe points out to him just before he recounts the fantasy, he has misheard the little boy sing "if a body *catch* a body":

> "It's 'If a body *meet* a body coming through the rye'!" old Phoebe said. "It's a poem. By Robert *Burns*." (156)

Holden answers: "I *know* it's a poem by Robert Burns." He knows the words, as would anyone his age at the time *The Catcher in the Rye* takes place. The song and its words were a standard tune of the day – of the sort sung around the piano at home. One understands that its words would come easily, and correctly, to the lips even of the little boy whom Holden mishears.

What, then, is the significance of Holden's error? The phrase "meet a body" conjures up not only a meeting between a lad and a lass, but because of the suggestiveness of "body" when detached from its Scottish meaning of "person," the phrase implies the coming together of male and female bodies. The next line of the song – "If a body kiss a body, need a body cry" – makes explicit the romantic/sexual context of the first. This is why Holden catches only the one line, and that one imperfectly. Unconsciously suppressing the word "meet," he avoids the very matter of his relations with girls, which he has been unable to resolve. "Meet" acts as another reminder, like the "Fuck you" graffiti that keep confronting him, of the disturbing sexual basis of love. Each time, Holden experiences a need to "erase" the reminder. And each time his need has reference to young people. The first graffito, after all, appears on a wall at his sister's school, and it is to protect youngsters that he is moved to erase it. His fantasy of rescue in the rye comes out of the same impulse to protect youngsters (and the youngster in himself) from vulgarized sexual knowledge.

Earlier, Holden has confronted the vulgarized kind of knowledge in his roommate Stradlater, who seems to have kissed a body: Jane Gallagher. To the question "if a body kiss a body need a body cry?" the answer, one may say, is "yes." For when Holden imagines not just a kiss but Stradlater and Jane having sex, he does end up "practically bawling" (after maneuvering Stradlater into beating him up). Once again he himself, having had a relationship with Jane that only once reached the stage of (chaste) kissing, is frozen at a painful stage of development. In contrast, Stradlater has, to Holden's dismay, broken through this stage. Accordingly, when Stradlater hints at having had sex with Jane, Holden takes a swing at him: "I told him he didn't even care if a girl kept all her kings in the back row or not." (42)

Holden has idealized Jane in a typical adolescent way, for "to adolescence proper belongs that unique experience, tender love," writes Peter Blos. But the adolescent boy must progress from an early "state of infatuation toward the fusion of tender and sexual love."[10] Having participated in Stradlater's splitting off of tender love from his sexual intentions toward Jane, Holden has maneuvered Stradlater into hitting him in order to be punished for this violation of Jane. The fusion of tender and sexual love remains difficult for Holden. It represents a vertiginous, dangerous kind of falling for him: the extreme of the suggestion contained in the words "falling in love."

The theme of falling extends from the catcher fantasy, to being knocked down by Stradlater, to the threat of falling off the curb while walking up Fifth Avenue (with the related threat of falling out of sanity and consciousness), to a series of trippings and pratfalls suffered by Holden in the course of his adventures. These falls convey adolescent sexual awkwardness – almost explicitly so when Holden trips over his suitcase on the way to letting a prostitute into his hotel room. Among 1940s romantic movie comedies, *The Lady Eve* makes explicit the pratfall's association with sexual awkwardness and excitation. In this movie, as Henry Fonda keeps falling in the presence of Barbara Stanwyck, it grows evident that his pratfalls anticipate his falling in love. That consummation is perhaps always a fall out of experience and control, and so always carries with it some of the fear of falling that troubles Holden.

Holden not only falls inadvertently in minor ways; he is repeatedly drawn toward catastrophic forms of falling. Each time, he is searching out self-punishment for his unconscious guilt over Allie's death. The wish to be punished by death accounts for his apparently illogical response to Phoebe's accusation that he doesn't like "*any*thing that's happening" (153). "I do!" he insists. But she challenges him to "name one thing." He has trouble "concentrating" on an answer, but then James Castle pops into his mind: this is a fellow student who leaped to his death. Clearly, Holden is half in love with easeful death.

At the same time, of course, he half hopes to be saved. On sneaking out of his parents' apartment after talking to Phoebe, he admits that "for some reason," at this point "I didn't give a damn any more if they caught me." Then, fixing on the word he has uttered, he adds: "I figured if they caught me, they caught me. I almost wished they did, in a way." (162) As much as he needs to fall, in other words, Holden needs to be caught. (Horsing around at school, he has expressed the same need. Pulling his cap down over his eyes, "I started groping around in front of me, like a blind guy. . . . I kept saying, 'Mother darling, why won't you give me your *hand?*' "[23])

Besides rescuing children from maturation, Holden may be said to be rescuing others in one further sense deriving from young love. "The sensitive adolescent who cannot yet fall in love with a specific person on a realistic basis," writes Theodore Lidz,

> . . . can experience a more diffuse love of nature or of mankind in which there is a vague seeking for expression and fulfillment of the feelings that are surging within him. He feels that he must lose himself in nature or find ways of giving himself in the service of mankind.[11]

The desire to serve mankind can lead to messianism, perhaps in the form of joining a cult or fringe political organization, or else it can eventuate in fantasies of service. In its negative form the same displacement of love leads to delinquency or running away from school. Holden moves in each of the negative directions, both running away and fantasizing himself a rescuer.

The phenomenon of adolescent messianism stands out as the single analytical conception actually referred to in *The Catcher in the Rye.* It is, in fact, the centerpiece of the one, serious, considered evaluation of Holden by another character – his former teacher, Antolini. In the course of an analysis of Holden that includes an emphasis on the imminence of his suffering some kind of "fall" (a usage that alerts the reader to a wide-ranging play on the meanings of this word), Antolini writes out for him some words "written by a psychoanalyst named Wilhelm Stekel": "The mark of the immature man is that he wants to die nobly for a cause, while the mark of the mature man is that he wants to live humbly for one" (170). The words capture the perfectionist urge in Holden, yet misrepresent him as leaning toward a messianism of action when actually his tendency is toward fantasies of rescue quite divorced from any social idea or cause.

The same distinction between action and fantasy applies to Holden's critique of society, which is sometimes taken to represent a reformist impulse, a wish for a better world. A careful scrutiny of Holden's dislikes, complaints, observations, and especially his generalizations about the world, however, reveals many of them to be personal. This is another way of saying that Holden is a first-person narrator of a particular kind. In novels with first-person narrators the common disparity is between the narrator's reports of what he observes (which are dependable) and his opinions (which are undependable). With Holden, there is additionally a range of reliability among his opinions depending on who and what he is evaluating.

Some of Holden's opinions prove to be merely selfish. Salinger exposes them by having Holden contradict himself through his own behavior. For example, he complains about his roommates and others only to repeat their annoying habits, like standing in the light.[12] Some of his complaints and generalizations – "people never give your message to anybody" (135) – betray a failure to notice that he is being patronized on account of his erratic behavior. Others are those of a spoiled prep school kid:

> I always get those vomity kind of cabs if I go anywhere late at night. (75)
>
> I hate living in New York and all. Taxicabs, and Madison Avenue buses, with the drivers and all always yelling at you to get out at the rear door, and being introduced to phony guys that call the Lunts angels, and going up and down in elevators when you just want to go outside, and guys fitting your pants all the time at Brooks, and people always . . . (118–19)

It is difficult to be sympathetic toward the frustrations of a youth who is privileged to ride in cabs and go to the theater. The act of exiting from the rear door of the bus to accommodate others hardly qualifies as a discontent of civilization. And if Holden expresses a boy's understandable uneasiness at being touched during a fitting, the fact that he is getting his clothes at Brooks Brothers undercuts sympathy with his complaint. In such passages even Holden's justly famous instinct for exposing phoniness appears personal and self-involved rather than socially oriented.

On the other hand, his observation of a woman who weeps over the sentimentalities of a movie while irritably refusing to take her child to the bathroom sharply exposes the contradiction in her behavior. This is the kind of feeling insight Holden is justly famous for. Projecting his own anxieties onto the child, as with the boy who inspired the catcher fantasy, his sensitivity to parental indifference here affords a sharp insight into the behavior of the mother.

Holden is insightful, it seems, where children are concerned, but less so with adults, especially parents (except when they are with their children). Similarly, he feels sympathy for the outcasts of life and literature – Hamlet, for example – but lacks sympathy for anyone who does not display a psychological disturbance – Romeo, for example. Thus Holden's own grappling with death gives him a certain insight into *Romeo and Juliet.* He speaks for many of those who have experienced the play, especially younger readers, when he picks Mercutio as his favorite character and expresses both disappointment and resentment at his being removed from the action so early.

Premature death has been Allie's fate as well, of course, and Holden understandably reacts with special urgency to any situation in which life goes on despite death. But Holden is less reliable when, again projecting his own guilt, he searches for scapegoats, as when he concludes that "it was Romeo's fault" that Mercutio died. He takes back the accusation, but then, yet again using the word "crazy," accounts for his response to the play in a passage that is really about Allie:

> The trouble is, it drives me crazy if somebody gets killed – especially somebody very smart and entertaining and all – and it's somebody else's fault.

Like Romeo, Holden is guilty because he has gone on living after Allie's death, and like Romeo he cannot really be accused of being at fault.

An examination of Holden's critique of society, then, shows him to be by turns merely irritable and positively insightful. Just as with the question of his sanity, there is evidence both for those who find him an admirable social critic and for those who do not. And once again the variability in question turns out to involve adolescent psychology – if not exclusively the realm of the adolescent moratorium. Taken as a whole, Holden's critique can be seen to relate to the sexually repressive component of his extended moratorium. His repression is manifested not only in his chaste relationship with Jane but also in his wish to become a monk, his preference for the two (nonsexual) nuns he meets over the other women, and his dismissal of the prostitute sent to his hotel room. As it happens, adolescent repression of sexuality, especially when tinged with an attraction to the ascetic, often produces exactly what Holden is known for: a tendency to deliver "negative judgments" on the world.[13]

If it has to be said that Holden's vision is often linked to personal and psychological sources, the feeling of most readers that he is somehow right about things in general cannot altogether be dismissed. Salinger himself has conveyed an impression of Holden's being right, possibly because he shifted in the course of writing from a noncommittal authorial distance to a perilously close identification with his protagonist. This shift can be observed when Holden's former teacher, Antolini, after somewhat inappropriately applying Wilhelm Stekel on messianism to Holden, goes on to employ a more persuasive formula: "You'll find," he tells him, "that you're not the first person who was ever confused and frightened and even sickened by human behavior." (170) The presumption expressed here that Holden is suffering from a kind of angst coincides with the attitude toward society usually taken by the critics who endorse Holden's vision.

Yet as his use of Stekel reveals, Antolini has only a general idea of what ails Holden. He has had a talk with Holden's father, but there is nothing to suggest that he has learned from it any more than that Holden has been flunking courses and seems disturbed. In the interview Antolini limits himself to discussing Holden's schoolwork. Inasmuch as he therefore has no way of knowing how the world impinges on Holden's consciousness, his explanations of Holden's behavior take on the aspect of authorial interpolations.

Salinger's attitude toward Antolini has always troubled readers. Antolini himself is eventually discredited. But his speech of analysis and advice – unlike that of the history teacher, Spencer, who also admonishes Holden to apply himself to his schoolwork – apparently is not discredited. On the other hand, his pronouncing Holden to have been "sickened by human behavior" and to be carrying an urge to reform society is certainly not accurate, however well it may describe the psychology of those readers who think they are seeing reflections of themselves, or their former selves, in *The Catcher in the Rye.* It seems, therefore, that as Salinger approached the end of his novel he began to draw uncritically close to his protagonist, and to betray that process through Antolini's philosophizing.

Salinger's slippage away from authorial distance starts at the beginning of the Antolini visit. Early in the conversation with his former teacher Holden gives a typically sensitive account of another outcast: the misfit fellow student who has been rebuked for repeatedly digressing when he delivers talks in Oral Expression. Holden likes digression, though, and regrets Mr. Vinson's giving the boy an *F* for his talk about the farm his father bought in Vermont – "because he hadn't told what kind of animals and vegetables and stuff grew on the farm and all." Holden is attracted to the idea that someone could "start out telling you about their father's farm and then all of a sudden get more interested in their uncle" (166). He is always attracted to defiance of fathers. But this is the one time when his critique, though spurred by personal identification, is in no way colored by its psychological source. His defense of digression has to be pronounced artistically sound. And the teacher who gives the *F,* unlike the other teachers in the book, is not technically right while being emotionally obtuse, but rather both wrong *and* obtuse. In contrast with everything that has gone before, then, Holden on digression is wholly justified in his rejection of the dogma of authority.

In the course of the Antolini scene, then, Salinger slides into becoming Holden's advocate and justifier, and a sentimentalized light is temporarily cast over Holden. One may speculate that the flaws in this much-analyzed scene are precisely the source of critical readings that lose *their* objectivity toward Holden. One may further speculate that Salinger sensed something wrong with the scene, and tried to correct it by later undercutting Antolini. But evidently because he was patching things up rather than writing out of a more purely creative impulse, he did so rather crudely by discrediting Antolini as a homosexual.

Except for this lapse, *The Catcher in the Rye* presents society and its figures of authority as both right and wrong. They are right that Holden's extended adolescent moratorium must come to an end, but surely wrong to dismiss him as a merely confused adolescent. For he is undergoing a special combination of kinds of mourning – for his brother Allie, for his own earlier childhood self, and for his parents as the revered figures of his youth – and his mourning has acted on his sensibility in strikingly creative ways. Such creativity, too, is a normal – if rare – accompaniment of adolescence.

As for Holden himself, he too is both right and wrong. He sometimes has exceptional insight into his world, and he sometimes suffers from skewed judgment. In turn, critics of *The Catcher in the Rye,* very much like the teachers and other figures of authority in the book, have also been both right and wrong. They have tended to overvalue Holden's insights, but have perhaps been right, after all, to treat his psychological disturbance as more normal than abnormal. The extreme verge of adolescent disturbance, after all, can be said both to approximate what would have to be diagnosed as psychosis in an adult, and to be a phase that can end in normalcy. Holden represents an extreme, but readers have sensed that he nevertheless connects with common experience.

Critics, common readers, the author of *The Catcher in the Rye* himself – all have found themselves drawn toward Holden. Some have reasoned that their attraction could be accounted for by the universality of his case, which they have taken to be essentially that of a normal teenager. Others have reasoned that, on the contrary, he is a special case: attractive precisely to the extent that his experience is not normal. But whether one is assessing Holden's sanity or his status as a social critic, the foregoing sketch of his psychology suggests that whoever wishes to hold an informed view of Holden Caulfield needs to take into account the peculiar patterns of adolescent crisis.

## NOTES

1. Diana Trilling, *Reviewing the Forties* (New York: Harcourt Brace Jovanovich, 1978), pp. 232, 218. See also "Growing Up in America: the 1940s and After," in Frederick R. Karl, *American Fictions 1940/1980* (New York: Harper & Row, 1983). On the weighting of critical opinion toward sympathy with Holden see James Bryan, "The Psychological Structure of *The Catcher in the Rye,*" PMLA 89 (1974): p. 1066.
2. Arthur Heiseman and James E. Miller, Jr., "J. D. Salinger: Some Crazy Cliff," *Western Humanities Review* (1956), reprinted in *If You Really Want to Know: A "Catcher" Casebook,* ed. Malcolm M. Marsden (Chicago: Scott, Foresman, 1963), p. 22.
3. Ernest Jones, review in *The Nation,* September 1, 1951, reprinted in *"Catcher" Casebook,* p. 9. An exception is a 1959 study in which

Holden is flatly pronounced "sick": Robert G. Jacobs, "J. D. Salinger's *The Catcher in the Rye:* Holden Caulfield's 'Goddam Autobiography'," *"Catcher" Casebook,* p. 62. See June Edwards, "Censorship in the Schools: What's Moral about *The Catcher in the Rye?" English Journal* 72 (April 1983): 39–42, for how Holden is still represented as a normally mixed-up teenager in high school classrooms.

4. E. H. Miller, "In Memoriam: Allie Cau[l]field in *The Catcher in the Rye," Mosaic: A Journal for the Interdisciplinary Study of Literature* 15 (Winter 1982): 129. See also Bryan, "The Psychological Structure."
5. This account of adolescence follows Anna Freud, as well as others cited below. More recent studies, without denying their account, "emphasize adaptive strengths and coping skills," and argue that the turmoil is less often the norm than is usually supposed. See Mark J. Blotcky and John G. Looney, "Normal Female and Male Adolescent Psychological Development: An Overview of Theory and Research," *Adolescent Psychiatry* 8 (1980): 196.
6. Holden also remarks that his grandmother "doesn't have all her marbles any more," and fixes on the song "It Was Just One of Those Things," the next line of which is: "just one of those *crazy* things." On the forty uses of "phony" see Robert A. Draffan, "Novel Approaches: Teaching *The Catcher in the Rye," The Use of English* 24 (Spring 1973): 203. The quotation from "I'm Crazy" is from *Collier's* (December 22, 1949): 36. The quotation from the novel ("she killed Allie, too") is from J. D. Salinger, *The Catcher in the Rye* (New York: New American Library, Signet ed., 1963), p. 64. All subsequent page references, appearing in parentheses in text, are to this edition.
7. Peter Blos, *On Adolescence: A Psychoanalytic Interpretation* (New York: The Free Press, 1962), p. 100; E. H. Miller, "In Memoriam," p. 129; Erik Erikson, "Youth: Fidelity and Diversity," in *The Challenge of Youth,* ed. Erik Erikson (Garden City, N.Y.: Doubleday Anchor, 1965 [rpt. of vol. of 1963]), pp. 13, 18.
8. On the tomb passage and purgation see Miller, "In Memoriam," 183–4. The range of ritual interpretations that have been proposed may be sampled in Gerald Rosen, "A Retrospective Look at *The Catcher in the Rye," American Quarterly* 29 (Winter 1977): 562, which concentrates on Holden in the rain after Phoebe's carousel ride; and in Carl F. Strauch, "Kings in the Back Row: Meaning Through Structure – A Reading of Salinger's *The Catcher in the Rye," Wisconsin Studies in Contemporary Literature* 2 (Winter 1961), in *"Catcher" Casebook,* p. 109, where "Central Park represents Holden's Dark Tower, Dark Night of the Soul, and Wasteland."

9. See Frederick L. Gwynn and Joseph L. Blotner, *The Fiction of J. D. Salinger,* (Pittsburgh: University of Pittsburgh Press, 1962), p. 30, cited by Bernard S. Oldsey, "The Movies in the Rye" (1961), in *"Catcher" Casebook,* p. 120; Rosen, "A Retrospective Look," p. 556; Strauch, "Kings in the Back Row," *"Catcher" Casebook,* p. 104. By getting Stradlater to mention the kings, it is suggested, Holden is sending Jane a warning to beware of Stradlater.
10. Blos, *Adolescence,* pp. 101, 102.
11. Theodore Lidz, *The Person: His Development Throughout the Life Cycle* (New York: Basic Books, 1968), p. 340.
12. Peter J. Seng, "The Fallen Idol: The Immature World of Holden Caulfield" (1961), in *"Catcher" Casebook,* p. 76.
13. Blos, *Adolescence,* p. 111.

# Notes on Contributors

*Christopher Brookeman* is Principal Lecturer in English and American Studies and Programme Director of the American Studies Resource Centre at the Polytechnic of Central London. He is the author of *American Culture and Society since the 1930s.*

*Michael Cowan,* a past president of the American Studies Association, is Professor of Literature and American Studies at the University of California, Santa Cruz. He is the author of *City of the West: Emerson, America, and Urban Metaphor.*

*Joyce Rowe* is an Assistant Professor of English at Fordham University. She is the author of *Equivocal Endings in Classic American Novels.*

*Jack Salzman,* the Director of the Center for American Culture Studies at Columbia University, is the editor of *Prospects: An Annual of American Culture Studies.* He also is coediting (with Charles Hamilton) the four-volume *Encyclopedia of African American Culture and History.*

*John Seelye* is Graduate Research Professor of American Literature at the University of Florida, Gainesville. Among his publications are *The True Adventures of Huckleberry Finn* and *Prophetic Waters: The River in Early American Life and Literature.*

*Peter Shaw* was most recently Will and Ariel Durant Professor of Humanities at St. Peter's College, Jersey City. He is the author of *The Character of John Adams* and *The War Against the Intellect: Episodes in the Decline of Discourse.*

# Selected Bibliography


Baumbach, Jonathan. "The Saint as a Young Man: *The Catcher in the Rye* by J. D. Salinger," in his *The Landscape of Nightmare: Studies in the Contemporary American Novel.* New York: New York University Press, 1965.

Bloom, Harold, ed. *J. D. Salinger: Modern Critical Views.* New York: Chelsea House, 1987.

Branch, Egar. "Mark Twain and J. D. Salinger: A Study in Literary Continuity." *American Quarterly* 9 (Summer 1957): 144–58.

French, Warren. *J. D. Salinger.* New York: Twayne, rev. ed. 1976; originally published 1963.

Geismar, Maxwell. "J. D. Salinger: The Wise Child and the *New Yorker* School of Fiction," in his *American Moderns: From Rebellion to Conformity.* New York: Hill and Wang, 1958.

Grunwald, Henry Anatole, ed. *Salinger: A Critical and Personal Portrait.* New York: Harper, 1962.

Gwynn, Frederick L. and Joseph L. Blotner. *The Fiction of J. D. Salinger.* Pittsburgh: University of Pittsburgh Press, 1958.

Hamilton, Ian. *In Search of J. D. Salinger.* New York: Random House, 1988.

Hamilton, Kenneth. *J. D. Salinger: A Critical Essay.* Grand Rapids, Mich.: William B. Erdmans, 1967.

Hassan, Ihab. "J. D. Salinger: Rare Quixotic Gesture," in his *Radical Innocence: The Contemporary American Novel.* Princeton, N.J.: Princeton University Press, 1961.

Heiserman, Arthur and James E. Miller, Jr. "J. D. Salinger: Some Crazy Cliff." *Western Humanities Review* 10 (Spring 1956): 129–37.

Lundquist, James. *J. D. Salinger.* New York: Fredrick Ungar, 1979.

Marsden, Malcolm M., ed. *If You Really Want to Know: A "Catcher" Casebook.* Chicago: Scott, Foresman, 1963.

*Modern Fiction Studies* 12 (Autumn 1966). Special Salinger number.

Ohmann, Carol and Richard Ohmann. "Reviewers, Critics, and *The Catcher in the Rye.*" *Critical Inquiry* 3 (Autumn 1976): 15–37.

Rosen, Gerald. "A Retrospective Look at *The Catcher in the Rye.*" *American Quarterly* 29 (Winter 1977): 547–62.

Salzberg, Joel, ed. *Critical Essays on Salinger's The Catcher in the Rye*. Boston: G. K. Hall, 1990.

Sublette, Jack R. *J. D. Salinger: An Annotated Bibliography, 1938–1981.* New York: Garland, 1984.

*Wisconsin Studies in Contemporary Literature* 4 (Winter 1963). Special Salinger number.